IMMIGRATION POLICY

Other Books in the At Issue Series:

IMMIGRATION POLICY

David Bender, *Publisher*

Bruno Leone, *Executive Editor*

Katie de Koster, *Managing Editor*

Scott Barbour, *Series Editor*

Scott Barbour, *Book Editor*

Greenhaven Press, Inc.
San Diego, California

Library of Congress Cataloging-in-Publication Data

At issue: immigration policy / book editor, Scott Barbour.
p.   cm. — (At issue series) (An opposing viewpoints series)
Includes bibliographical references and index.
ISBN 1-56510-267-3 (pbk.) — ISBN 1-56510-300-9 (lib.).
1. United States—Emigration and immigration—Government policy. 2. Refugees—Legal status, laws, etc.—United States. 3. Emigration and immigration law—United States. [1. United States—Emigration and immigration.] I. Barbour, Scott, 1963-   . II. Title: Immigration policy. III. Series. IV. Series: Opposing viewpoints series (Unnumbered)
JV6455.5.A8   1995   94-28149
325.73—dc20   CIP
                                                                          AC

© 1995 by Greenhaven Press, Inc., PO Box 289009,
San Diego, CA 92198-9009

Printed in the U.S.A.

Table of Contents

Introduction

In August 1993, California governor Pete Wilson published a full-page "open letter to the President of the United States" in newspapers nationwide in which he addressed the issue of immigration. In the letter, Wilson complained that his state was paying a high price for the failure of the federal government—which bears sole authority over immigration—to control the nation's borders. He called for a repeal of the federal mandates that require state governments to pay the costs for the education, health care, and incarceration of illegal immigrants. Furthermore, he proposed amending the Constitution to deny citizenship to the U.S.-born children of illegal immigrants.

Numerous commentators objected to Wilson's approach. Some criticized it as a manipulative attempt to garner political support. According to Barbara Jordan, chairperson of a federal immigration review commission, "It's a given fact that the electoral fortunes of the governor of California as he seeks re-election [in 1994] are enhanced by his pronouncements on immigration." Others considered Wilson's comments part of a growing trend on the part of politicians and the public to unfairly blame immigrants for society's ills and to strip them of their human and civil rights. The immigrant rights group La Resistencia, for example, described Wilson's letter as "a lesson in scapegoating of the ugliest and most mean-spirited style" that constituted "a call for ethnic cleansing—U.S. Style!"

While critics objected to Wilson's tone, many people agreed with the substance of his message on immigration. For example, George B. High, executive director of the Center for Immigration Studies, argues that immigrants are largely responsible for California's poor economy, increasing racial tensions, and decaying environmental conditions. He writes that Wilson "has been severely criticized by immigrant advocacy groups who claim he is 'scapegoating' and blaming all California's woes on immigrants. The realities of life in the state, however, undermine this claim." Californians themselves appear to agree with High. A 1993 poll by the *Los Angeles Times* found that 69 percent of Californians considered illegal immigration to be a serious problem, 54 percent favored changing the Constitution to deny citizenship to U.S.-born children of illegal immigrants, 73 percent favored using the National Guard to control the U.S.-Mexico border, 39 percent favored prohibiting illegal immigrants from attending public schools, and 23 percent favored denying emergency health care to illegal immigrants.

A heated argument

Discussions on immigration are often heated. Wilson's letter and the responses it provoked from immigrant advocates and opponents illustrate the divisiveness of the debate. Opponents of immigration charge that America is being "invaded" by immigrants—legal and illegal—who threaten American society. Immigrant advocates respond that attacks on immigrants are unfair and often racist. Amid the din of conflicting opinions, studies on how immigration affects the economy are used as weapons by all sides.

While the contemporary immigration debate conveys a sense of immediacy, however, each faction of the battle has roots in America's history. Early popular movements to curtail immigration expressed the same fears of social fragmentation and economic decline that characterize contemporary arguments against immigration. Moreover, contemporary advocates of liberal immigration policies hearken back to an era, prior to the mid-nineteenth century, when immigration was entirely unregulated. These continuities between past and present suggest that besides being "a nation of immigrants," America is a country that argues about immigration.

Cultural opposition

One faction in the contemporary immigration debate holds that large numbers of immigrants—especially from the Third World—threaten to disunite American society and culture. For example, Republican commentator Pat Buchanan regrets that immigration is changing the ethnic composition of the nation, a change that he believes contributes to increasing racial tensions and cultural fragmentation. He writes that due to immigration, "By 2050, . . . whites may be near a minority in an America of 81 million Hispanics, 62 million blacks and 41 million Asians. . . . The United States will have become a veritable Brazil of North America."

While Buchanan's views may seem extreme, and are indeed offensive to many Americans, they are not new. The first restrictions on immigration to America were created in response to similar concerns. For example, in 1882, to appease popular intolerance of Chinese immigrants in California, Congress passed the Chinese Exclusion Act. Another major piece of legislation, the Quota Act of 1921, was designed to preserve the nation's predominately northern and western European ethnic composition by decreasing immigration from southern and eastern Europe.

Economic arguments

However, rather than deploring immigration's effects on the nation's ethnic composition (an argument that is often attacked as racist), most immigration opponents argue that immigration harms the U.S. economy. These critics contend that by increasing the supply of labor and settling for lower pay, immigrants take jobs from U.S.-born workers and drive down the wages of those who retain their jobs. Moreover, they commonly assert that immigrants pay less in taxes than they receive in the form of social service benefits. These critics point to numerous studies to back up their position. For example, a 1994 study by economist Donald L. Huddle of Rice University in Houston, Texas, calculates the net national costs of immigration—including the cost of unemployment benefits for U.S.-born workers displaced by immigrants. He concludes that in 1992, immigrants cost the nation $42.5 billion more than they paid in taxes.

These economic objections to immigration, like cultural opposition, have roots in the past. Concern about the effects of immigration on U.S.-born workers was evident in the 1800s. According to the *CQ Researcher*, a weekly news and research publication, "Early immigration laws . . . responded to calls by the burgeoning labor movement to protect American jobs and wages." Moreover, the fear that immigrants would become dependent on welfare also motivated early lawmakers. One of the first immigration laws was designed to exclude the entry of people likely to become a "public Charge."

Economic proponents

While some see immigration as a threat to the economy, others view it as a benefit. This opinion is widely accepted by free-market economists who believe that goods and labor should be allowed to flow freely across international borders. Thus the *Wall Street Journal* has consistently advocated a policy of "open borders," and business leaders and libertarians often propose liberal immigration policies. These people point to studies indicating that immigrants do not displace U.S.-born workers, depress wages, or abuse social services. Julian L. Simon, a leading proponent of this perspective and the author of *The Economic Consequences of Immigration*, insists that immigrants—whether legal or illegal—do not adversely affect U.S. workers. He writes that "immigration does not exacerbate unemployment. . . . Immigrants not only take jobs, but also create them. Their purchases increase the demand for labor, leading to new hires roughly equal in number to the immigrant workers." Simon also rejects the contention that immigrants strain social service budgets. Rather, he contends, they "contribute more to the public coffers in taxes than they draw out in welfare services."

The idea that immigration is good for the country's economy has roots in early America's liberal immigration policy. Indeed, in the first century of the nation's history, immigration went unregulated. According to the *CQ Researcher*, this lack of restriction reflected "the need for more people to drive the economy and carry out the westward expansion." As is commonly noted, immigrants helped build America's infrastructure. For example, until 1882, when the Chinese Exclusion Act suspended the immigration of Chinese laborers, immigrants from China were welcomed for their help constructing the country's first transcontinental railroad, which was completed in 1869.

A nation of immigrants

Other advocates of liberal policies support immigration for ideological reasons. For example, many celebrate America's history as a nation of immigrants and support the continuation of this tradition, which they believe has created a society rich in diverse cultural attributes.

The conviction that open immigration makes a positive contribution to America's pluralistic society was overridden by Congress in 1921 when it passed the Quota Act, which effectively limited the entry of certain nationalities—particularly those of southern and eastern Europe. Limitation on immigration by country of origin remained the law for over forty years: Congress followed up the Quota Act with the National Origins Act of 1924, which limited immigrants from outside the Western Hemisphere, and the Immigration and Naturalization Act of 1952, which set limited quotas for Asian countries. But in the early 1960s, President John F. Kennedy sharply criticized this policy, arguing that "the national origins quota system has strong overtones of an indefensible racial preference." Two years after Kennedy's assassination, liberal politicians succeeded in abolishing racial preferences when they passed the Immigration Act of 1965.

Immigrant rights advocates

Perhaps the most vocal supporters of immigrants are immigrant rights advocates. This faction consists of individuals and groups who speak out against perceived abuses of immigrants' rights. For example, in 1992, the human rights group Americas Watch issued a report entitled *Brutality Unchecked*, which documents cases of physical, verbal, and sexual abuse of immigrants allegedly committed by agents of the U.S. Border Patrol, the law enforcement arm of the Immigration and Naturalization Service (INS). Besides monitoring human rights, these advocates also protest policies that they say violate immigrants' civil rights. For example, they oppose the employer sanctions provision of the Immigration Reform and Control Act of 1986 (IRCA), which imposes fines on employers who knowingly hire illegal immigrants. Opponents of this law argue that it deprives illegal immigrants of their basic right to work, earn a living, and provide for their families. Moreover, critics point out, even the U.S. General Accounting Office has concluded that IRCA causes discrimination against minorities because employers, fearing fines, are reluctant to hire anyone who looks foreign.

The twentieth century has seen various advocacy efforts on behalf of immigrants. For example, in the early 1900s, "settlement houses"—community centers established to combat inner-city social problems—helped immigrants adjust to their new country and formed immigrant protective organizations. In the early 1960s, farm worker Cesar Chavez began organizing a union for California grape pickers, many of whom were migrants from Mexico. Chavez's union, which eventually grew to become the United Farm Workers of America (UFW), was credited with improving the working and living conditions of migrant farm workers in California, Arizona, Texas, and Florida.

"What makes America America"

The activities of immigrant rights advocates reveal that the immigration debate is not merely an abstract argument about economics or ideology. Immigration policies affect people—both immigrants and U.S.-born residents. Consequently, a person's beliefs about immigration are often intensely personal and not easily altered. As *New Republic* editor Michael Kinsley writes, "Immigration is a subject on which very few opinions are changed because of arguments or statistics. Your views on immigration depend on your sense of what makes America America." In *At Issue: Immigration Policy*, various commentators express their visions of America as they discuss and debate the topic of immigration.

1

Immigration Policy:
A Historical Overview

The CQ Researcher

The CQ Researcher *is a weekly news and research publication of Congressional Quarterly Inc.*

Prior to the mid-nineteenth century, few restrictions were placed on immigration as immigrants helped build the infrastructure and fuel the economy of an expanding new nation. The first immigration quotas were established to appease rising nativist sentiments in the late nineteenth century. Since then, immigration policies have evolved in response to various foreign policy developments and domestic economic situations.

The United States—indeed, the whole Western Hemisphere—has been peopled by immigrants. The Asian ancestors of Native Americans arrived first, crossing the land bridge that linked Russia and Alaska sometime between 25,000 B.C. and 10,000 B.C. By the time European explorers discovered the hemisphere in the late 15th century, these early immigrants had settled throughout North and South America.

During the Colonial period, most immigrants came from Northern Europe, mainly Britain, France, Scandinavia and the Netherlands. In addition, about a half-million Africans were brought to the Colonies as slaves. After the Revolutionary War ended in 1781, immigrants began pouring into the new country.

The Founding Fathers worried about the impact of immigration. Thomas Jefferson feared that immigrants from countries still ruled by kings might undermine the new republic's political foundations, while George Washington and the Federalists worried that new immigrants might lean too far in the opposite direction and challenge the federal government's powers. But the need for more people to drive the economy and carry out the westward expansion outweighed such concerns. Consequently, a specific policy governing immigration didn't emerge until the 20th century.

Until then, a few minor laws governed immigration. Since the early 19th century, ship captains had been required to collect and submit information on immigrants they brought to the United States. Newcomers

"Immigration Reform," *The CQ Researcher*, September 24, 1993. Reprinted with permission.

became naturalized citizens after five years of residence by declaring their intent before witnesses in a state court. The requirements were good moral character and loyalty to the principles of the Constitution.[1]

Rise of opposition

As long as the expanding nation needed immigrants, national policy on immigration remained scant. Then came the next wave of European immigration, which continued for most of the 1800s. This group included settlers from throughout Europe, including desperately impoverished Irish peasants, Germans fleeing revolution, and people from Austria-Hungary, Italy, Greece, Russia and Turkey. Generally less skilled than earlier immigrants, they were drawn by the promise of employment in American factories. Most settled near their ports of entry, New York and Philadelphia. At the same time, French Canadians came to New England to work in the textile mills.

The sudden arrival of some 5 million newcomers between 1820 and 1860—many of whom were Catholic and did not speak English—sparked anti-immigrant sentiment among the predominantly Protestant Anglo-Saxon populations of the Northeastern cities where most new immigrants settled. These "nativist" sentiments exploded in violence in some cities, notably Philadelphia, where a three-day riot occurred in 1844.

Anti-immigrant sentiment gave rise to the Native American Party in the 1850s. Also called the Know Nothing Party (after its members' refusal to answer questions about their political activities), the movement drew support primarily from native-born workers who felt the new immigrants threatened their job security and religion, as well as the American political system. During its brief heyday in the 1850s, the Know Nothings enjoyed substantial support in Massachusetts and other Northeastern states.[2]

Congressional response

Congress responded with the 1882 Immigration Act, for the first time defining national immigration policy. In addition to declaring immigration regulation a task of the federal government, the law barred those who seemed likely to require special public services, including ex-convicts and the mentally ill.

At the same time that Catholic Europeans were pouring into East Coast cities, immigration from Asia was rising in the West. Most of the 42,000 Asians who arrived in the 1850s came from China and settled in California. Fleeing revolution and famine at home, they were drawn by a high demand for labor on the transcontinental railroad and later in mines and service businesses.

Chinese immigrants met with perhaps more resistance than their European counterparts in the East. In 1882, Congress bowed to anti-immigrant pressure in California and passed the first Chinese exclusion law, which set a quota on the number of Chinese immigrants admitted each year. The law remained on the books until 1943. Before the U.S. Supreme Court struck down all state laws restricting immigration in 1875, California also imposed a fee on Chinese immigrants coming in and other measures aimed at curbing immigration.

Subsequent federal laws expanded the list of unwelcome, or "excludable," immigrants to include polygamists, people convicted of crimes of moral turpitude and those with contagious diseases, such as cholera and tuberculosis. In 1903, the list grew even longer, banning anarchists, epileptics, the insane and "professional beggars."[3]

Early immigration laws also responded to calls by the burgeoning labor movement to protect American jobs and wages. In the 1880s, Congress prohibited employers from importing large numbers of low-wage contract workers whose presence pushed down wages throughout an industry or area where contract labor was common.

A specific policy governing immigration didn't emerge until the 20th century.

To administer the growing array of immigration regulations, Congress in 1891 created the Office of Immigration within the Treasury Department. In 1906, the office was given responsibility for naturalization, renamed the Bureau of Immigration and Naturalization and shifted to the Commerce and Labor Department. The 1906 Naturalization Act also tightened the conditions of citizenship by requiring applicants to speak English and sign their applications.

The new regulations reflected public concern over the continued surge of immigrants into the 20th century. From 1900 to 1920, 14.5 million people arrived in the United States, exceeding a million in some years. The majority of these new arrivals came from Italy, Russia and Austria-Hungary. Anti-immigrant sentiment mounted as the economy stagnated, prompting Congress to pass—over President Woodrow Wilson's veto—the 1917 Immigration Act. It reiterated all the exclusions enumerated by previous legislation, required that all immigrants be able to read and write and barred most Asians and Pacific Islanders.

Postwar hostility

After falling during World War I, immigration from war-ravaged Europe soared after 1920. But hostility toward new immigrants mounted even further with economic stagnation, high unemployment and a housing shortage. In response, Congress passed the 1921 Quota Act. In addition to restricting the number of new immigrants for the first time, the new law was designed to maintain the country's ethnic and cultural status quo. It did so by creating the national origins system, which set an annual limit on the number of admissible immigrants of a given nationality at 3 percent of their numbers already living in the United States. A subsequent law required immigrants to obtain visas from U.S. embassies in their countries before they left for the United States.

Because many more Americans at the time hailed from "old" immigrant countries of Northern and Western Europe than from other parts of the world, the new law made immigration much more difficult for such newcomers as Italians, Spaniards or Russians, not to mention Asians or Africans. The new restrictions prompted the first significant illegal immigration by excluded Europeans, who entered the country via Mexico or Canada, which were not subject to quota limits. The bureau responded to this new problem in 1924 by creating the Border Patrol.

Immigration plummeted during the 1930s as the Depression eliminated American job opportunities. At the same time, applications for refugee status grew throughout the decade with the rise to power of Adolf

Hitler and the persecution of Jews and other minorities in Germany and the countries under Nazi occupation. But because of the Quota Act's national limits, relatively few of these refugees could enter the United States.

During World War II, national security concerns influenced immigration policy, further reducing new arrivals. The 1940 Alien Registration Act required the fingerprinting and registration of all new immigrants and mandated deportation of criminals and subversives. Anti-Japanese sentiment sparked by fears of a Japanese invasion after the bombing of Pearl Harbor prompted the internment of thousands of Japanese Americans, many of whom were not recent immigrants but second- or third-generation U.S. citizens.

World War II also saw the introduction of a new program to offset labor shortages caused by the draft. Beginning in 1942, foreigners were permitted to enter the United States for temporary work. Most came from Mexico and harvested crops during the agricultural season before returning home. Because wages were much lower in Mexico than in the United States, growers were able to pay these temporary workers much less than American citizens. The 1951 U.S.-Mexican Migrant Labor Agreement made the popular Bracero program, as it was called, permanent. It was finally discontinued in 1964. Other wartime laws eliminated racial exclusions embodied in earlier measures and made it possible for immigrants from China, India and the Philippines to become naturalized citizens.

Policy reforms

Before the 1940s, the United States had no system to deal separately with refugees. In the wake of World War II, however, a wave of refugees from the devastation in Europe appealed for entry into the United States. Under the 1948 Displaced Persons Act, Congress set up a refugee system separate from the apparatus governing immigration, which over the next four years admitted almost 400,000 refugees.

Congress extended the program in the early 1950s to accommodate people fleeing communist countries outside the quota system, mainly Cuba and Hungary. Many of the refugees were given status as permanent residents, enabling them to become naturalized citizens. At the same time, the outbreak of the Cold War and its attendant anti-communism led to the exclusion of aliens suspected of communist leanings.

Meanwhile, drastic changes in immigration patterns and concerns over national interest led Congress to overhaul the entire immigration and naturalization system. A new law, the 1952 Immigration and Nationality Act, incorporated many of the changes introduced since the 1930s, including national quotas and alien registration. The measure became law only after Congress overrode a veto by President Harry S Truman, who joined many lawmakers in opposing the quota and registration provisions. The new law also broke new ground by setting up preference categories favoring skilled workers and relatives of citizens and resident aliens.

A decade later, lawmakers heeded Truman's objections. Supporters of immigration reform, including President John F. Kennedy, criticized the racial and ethnic preferences embodied in the national quota system. Calls for change mounted with the spread of the civil rights movement. Finally, in 1965, Congress abolished the national origins quota system. In its place, numerical limits were set on the basis of preference categories giving priority to relatives of citizens or permanent residents and to immigrants who possessed skills needed by industry. Refugees also were granted preference status and folded into the general immigration system. When the new limits took effect in 1968, an annual quota of 170,000 entrants from the Eastern Hemisphere was set.

> *Early immigration laws . . . responded to calls by the burgeoning labor movement to protect American jobs and wages.*

Immigration from the Western Hemisphere, meanwhile, had become a problem after the Bracero program ended. Immigrants had continued to pour in from Mexico and South and Central America, lured by the booming U.S. economy. To slow the flow, Congress in 1968 set the first annual quota for immigration from the Western Hemisphere, at 120,000.

Together with the termination of the Bracero program in 1964, the new quotas actually increased illegal immigration. Once limited largely to drug smugglers and immigrants from quota nations, illegal immigration grew to include farm workers who had become accustomed to migrating seasonally and other citizens from the Western Hemisphere who had enjoyed unlimited entry before 1968. As political and economic conditions throughout the hemisphere deteriorated in the 1970s and '80s, illegal immigration continued to grow despite enhanced enforcement by the Border Patrol, the enforcement arm of the Immigration and Naturalization Service (INS).

Recent legislation

The abolition of national origins quotas in 1965 changed the largely European face of immigration to the United States. Initially, refugees from Cuba and, after the Vietnam War, Southeast Asia diversified the immigrant pool. Political unrest in Central America in the late 1970s and '80s added Latinos to the mix. To meet these changing circumstances, Congress passed three major immigration laws.

The 1980 Refugee Act placed the new refugees outside the general preference system and set limits on the number to be admitted each year. The law also established procedures for granting permanent-resident status to a certain number of refugees each year.

In addition to the plight of refugees, illegal immigration continued to plague officials throughout the 1980s. In 1986, Congress attacked the problem from a new front—the demand side. The sweeping Immigration Reform and Control Act (IRCA) prohibited employers from hiring undocumented aliens. Employers were required to verify their workers' eligibility for employment and could be fined up to $10,000 for violations. IRCA also addressed the supply side of illegal immigration by granting an amnesty to all undocumented aliens who could prove they had lived in the United States since before Jan. 1, 1982. The law gave temporary-resident status to eligible residents, who could later become permanent residents.

A third recent law overhauled policies governing legal immigration. The 1990 Immigration Act changed the preference categories while at the same time increasing the number of immigrants allowed into the United States each year. Preferences are given to relatives of U.S. citizens and resident aliens and to "priority" workers, such as noteworthy university professors, researchers, executives and professionals and their immediate relatives.

Notes

1. See Vernon M. Briggs Jr., *Immigration Policy and the American Labor Force* (1984), p. 19.

2. *Ibid.*, p. 22.

3. Immigration and Naturalization Service, *An Immigrant Nation: United States Regulation of Immigration, 1798-1991* (June 18, 1991), p. 5. The remainder of this section is based on this INS publication, unless otherwise noted.

2

Immigration to the United States Should Be Reduced

George F. Kennan

George F. Kennan is an American diplomat and foreign policy expert. He is well known for developing the U.S. policy of containment in response to Soviet expansionism following World War II. Author of numerous books on foreign policy and U.S.-Soviet relations, he served as ambassador to the Soviet Union in 1952 and as ambassador to Yugoslavia from 1961 to 1963.

Although the United States is traditionally a nation of immigrants, current social conditions demonstrate that there are limits to the number of people the country can accommodate. A continued dependence on cheap labor imported from poverty-stricken countries threatens to re-create Third World conditions in the United States. Immigration should be reduced in order to preserve America's environment, culture, and prosperity relative to less developed countries.

Ours is, of course, a country of immigrants. In the pedigree of every non–Native American, other than the first-generation ones, there lies at least one immigrant, often a considerable number of them. We could justly be called an immigrant society.

We have prided ourselves, throughout much of our history, on the welcome we gave to the arriving immigrant, and even on the lack of discrimination we showed in the extension of this welcome. We have gone on the assumption that such were the spaciousness and fertility and the absorbent capacities of this country that there was no limit to either the number or the diversity of ethnic characteristics of the immigrants we could accept. We have gone on the further assumption that such was the universality of the values incorporated into our political system that there could be no immigrant, of whatever culture or race or national tradition, who could not be readily absorbed into our social and political life, could not become infused with understanding for, and confidence in, our political institutions, and could not, consequently, become a useful bearer of the American political tradition. Particularly has the possibility never become apparent to us that in some instances, where the disparity between what these people were leaving behind and what they were coming into was too great, the new arrivals, even in the process of adjusting to our political tradition, might actually change it. One need only look at our great-city ghettos or the cities of Miami and Los Angeles to satisfy oneself that what we are confronted with here are real and extensive cultural changes.

I shall not argue about how justifiable these attitudes proved to be in the past. Perhaps there was more to be said for some of them in the early days of this republic than there would be today. But, in any case, that is water over the dam. We must look at these assumptions in terms of the situation we now have before us.

Where are the limits?

If there are any grounds for my belief that the country is already over-populated—overpopulated, above all, from the environmental stand-point—then that would in itself suggest that we should take a new look at the whole problem of immigration. But we also ought to ask ourselves, before we assure ourselves that we could comfortably accommodate further waves of immigration, where, if anywhere, the limits of this complacency are to be found. This is a big world. Billions—rapidly increasing billions—of people live outside our borders. Obviously, a great number of them, being much poorer than they think most of us are, look enviously over those borders and would like, if they could, to come here.

Just as water seeks its own level, so relative prosperity, anywhere in the world, tends to suck in poverty from adjacent regions to the lowest levels of employment. But since poverty is sometimes a habit, sometimes even an established way of life, the more prosperous society, by indulging this tendency, absorbs not only poverty into itself but other cultures in the bargain, and is sometimes quite overcome, in the long run, by what it has tried to absorb. The inhabitants of the onetime Italian cities along the eastern shore of the Adriatic Sea (the scenes of some of Shakespeare's plays) made it a habit, over several centuries, to take their menial servants and their ditchdiggers from the Slavs of the poorer villages in the adjacent mountains. Today, finally, the last of the Italians have left; and the beautiful cities in question are inhabited entirely by Slavs, who have little relationship to the sort of city and the cultural monuments they have inherited. They have simply displaced the original inhabitants.

Surely there is a lesson in this. The situation has been, or threatens to be, repeated in a number of the advanced countries. It is obviously easier, for the short run, to draw cheap labor from adjacent pools of poverty, such as North Africa or Central America, than to find it among one's own people. And to the millions of such prospective immigrants from poverty to prosperity, there is, rightly or wrongly, no place that looks more attractive than the United States. Given its head, and subject to no restrictions, this pressure will find its termination only when the levels of overpopulation and poverty in the United States are equal to those of the countries from which these people are now so anxious to escape.

There will be those who will say, "Oh, it is our duty to receive as many as possible of these people and to share our prosperity with them, as we have so long been doing." But suppose there are limits to our capacity to absorb. Suppose the effect of such a policy is to create, in the end, conditions within this country no better than those of the places the mass of the immigrants have left: the same poverty, the same distress. What we shall then have accomplished is not to have appreciably improved conditions in the Third World (for even the maximum numbers we could conceivably take would be only a drop from the bucket of the planet's overpopulation) but to make this country itself a part of the Third World (as certain parts of it already are), thus depriving the planet of one of the few great regions that might have continued, as it now does, to be helpful to much of the remainder of the world by its relatively high standard of civilization, by its quality as example, by its ability to shed insight on the problems of the others and to help them find their answers to their own problems.

Actually, the inability of any society to resist immigration, the inability to find other solutions to the problem of employment at the lower, more physical, and menial levels of the economic process, is a serious weakness, and possibly even a fatal one, in any national society. The fully healthy society would find ways to meet those needs out of its own resources. The acceptance of this sort of dependence on labor imported from outside is, for the respective society, the evidence of a lack of will—in a sense, a lack of confidence in itself. And this acceptance, like the weakness of the Romans in allowing themselves to become dependent on the barbarians to fill the ranks of their own armies, can become, if not checked betimes, the beginning of the end.

The inability of any society to resist immigration . . . is a serious weakness, and possibly even a fatal one, in any national society.

However one cuts it, the question is not whether there are limits to this country's ability to absorb immigration; the question is only where those limits lie, and how they should be determined and enforced— whether by rational decision at this end or by the ultimate achievement of some sort of a balance of misery between this country and the vast pools of poverty elsewhere that now confront it.

A lack of vigor

Unfortunately it appears, as things stand today, to lie beyond the vigor, and the capacity for firm decision, of the American political establishment to draw any rational limits to further immigration. This is partly because the U.S. government, while not loath to putting half a million armed troops into the Middle East to expel the armed Iraqis from Kuwait, confesses itself unable to defend its own southwestern border from illegal immigration by large numbers of people armed with nothing more formidable than a strong desire to get across it. But behind this rather strange helplessness there lie, of course, domestic-political pressures or inhibitions that work in the same direction: notably, the thirst for cheap labor among American employers and the tendency of recently immigrated people, now here in such numbers that they are not without political clout, to demand the ongoing admission of others like themselves.

Let me make it clear that I am not objecting, here, to the quality of the people whose continued arrival, as things now stand, is to be anticipated (although I would point out that the conditions in our major urban ghettos would suggest that there might even be limits to our capacity for assimilation). We are already, for better or for worse, very much a polyglot country; and nothing of that is now to be changed. What I have in mind here are sheer numbers. There *is* such a thing as overcrowding. It has its psychic effects as well as its physical ones. There *are* limits to what the environment can stand: the tolerable levels of pollution, the strain on water supplies, and so on. There *are* limits to the desirable magnitude of urbanization; and it is, after all, to the great urban regions that the bulk of these immigrants proceed.

3

The United States Should Enact a Moratorium on Immigration

Dan Stein

Dan Stein is the executive director of the Federation for American Immigration Reform (FAIR), a Washington, D.C., organization that advocates greater restrictions on immigration.

An ongoing influx of immigrants to the United States is causing excessive population growth, cultural fragmentation, ethnic tension, and declining living standards. In order to reverse these trends, immigration should be halted until the government formulates more restrictive immigration policies.

Recent public opinion polls show that Americans are becoming more concerned about immigration. According to a recent Roper poll, 55 percent of the respondents support a temporary moratorium on all legal immigration, except for spouses and minor children of U.S. citizens.

A moratorium—a temporary freeze in immigration—may sound like a radical proposal. Given their support for the idea, most Americans apparently accept the concept. Many ideas that seemed radical just a few years ago are suddenly finding new acceptance at a time when many Americans believe the political process is spinning out of control. From the concept of a balanced budget amendment, to term limitations for members of Congress, to possibly electing a third party candidate [H. Ross Perot] for president, Americans are voicing their dissatisfaction with a political process that has lost touch with the people.

New census data from 1990 reveal that immigration is a major contributor to U.S. population growth, reshaping the culture and character of our nation, and is a partial factor in the growing gap between rich and poor. As a result of an unprecedented wave of immigration over the last 30 years, the United States now has the greatest foreign-born population in our history. And there is no end in sight. Changes made in the immigration laws in 1990 mean that today's foreign-born population of 20 million will grow to at least 30 million by the year 2000.

Dan Stein, "Why America Needs a Moratorium on Immigration," *The Social Contract*, Fall 1992. Reprinted with permission.

The stress of this unending influx is beginning to take its toll. The riots in Los Angeles [in the spring of 1992], and growth projections for California as a whole, present a compelling case that, right now, America is unprepared for more people. Our schools, housing, employment, living standards and deteriorating infrastructure demand a short pause in immigration.

The idea is not new. In the 18th and 19th centuries, immigration waves were short and modest. They often corresponded to acute, short-term situations. But in the 20th century, the situation is different. The huge wave that began in 1890 started with cheap steamer fares and recruitment by labor contractors. It ended in 1921 only because Congress finally imposed limits [the Quota Act] that curtailed immigration substantially.

> *The United States now has the greatest foreign-born population in our history.*

As noted immigration historian John Higham and Sloan Foundation expert Michael Teitelbaum have recently observed, the lull in immigration beginning with 1920 and continuing through the mid-1960s provided the breathing space that enabled the newcomers in that large wave to assimilate and prosper.

An immigration moratorium now would provide an opportunity to examine what has happened to this society in the past three decades of massive, unprecedented legal and illegal immigration. We must then move toward establishing immigration policies which will allow us to stabilize our population, halt the decline in American living standards, and reduce the increasingly divisive cultural fragmentation and ethnic tension.

Immigration to the United States in all forms now surpasses 1 million annually. Nearly 3 million are on waiting lists abroad for visas to enter permanently. A recent study by the Census Bureau found that there are 20 million immediate relatives of American citizens and resident aliens who are potentially eligible for entry with an immigration preference. A 1989 *Los Angeles Times* poll in Mexico found that 4.7 million Mexicans—about 6 percent of their population of 85 million—intended to emigrate to the United States.

An overloaded system

All indicators show that the U.S. migrant intake system is overloaded, and is easily manipulated by fraud and deceit. Using phony documents and false claims, immigrants routinely are able to create delays and outwit overburdened hearing examiners. False claims of U.S. citizenship are nearly impossible to detect, while those who overstay visas can easily remain in the U.S. indefinitely.

Worldwide demand for settlement in the United States will escalate in the 1990s. The Third World's labor force will expand by half-a-billion job seekers in the next decade, and will look beyond the borders of their economically underdeveloped countries for economic hope. Millions of earlier immigrants will bring in family members, and political and social unrest abroad will generate millions more refugees worldwide. Like a chain letter, an initial trickle turns into a stream that becomes a river and then a flood. Like shoveling snow in a blizzard, the more rapidly immigrants are admitted by a beleaguered INS [Immigration and Naturalization Service], the faster grows the backlog of relatives waiting to enter.

Because all efforts by Congress to solve these problems have quickly collapsed under intense special interest pressure, America needs a three-year moratorium to:

- reduce illegal immigration;
- implement and improve a national documents protocol to verify work eligibility;
- revise immigration laws to reduce substantially overall numbers (to around 300,000 annually); and
- complete a comprehensive analysis of the long-term effects of future immigration and population growth on the demography, the environment, and the cultural and employment/economic resources of our country.

Ultimately, we need to answer this question: what should be the purpose of immigration, now and in the future?

Until we answer that basic question, a moratorium on immigration may be the only option we have left.

4

The Federal Government Should Increase Control of Illegal Immigration

Pete Wilson

Pete Wilson was elected governor of California in 1990. He formerly served as a U.S. senator and as the mayor of San Diego, California.

The failure of the U.S. government to control illegal immigration places an unfair economic burden on state governments—especially that of California—that are required to provide social services to illegal immigrants. To remove the incentives for illegal immigration, the federal government should take the following steps: stop forcing state governments to provide education, health care, and other benefits to illegal immigrants; create an identification system to assure that government benefits are provided only to legal residents; and amend the Constitution to deny U.S. citizenship to children born in the United States of illegal immigrant parents.

This year [1994], California faces yet another enormous budget crisis, badly exacerbated by both the policies and the inaction of the federal government.

Defense cuts, environmental decisions, and tax hikes coming from Washington are all hurting California's economy. But nothing is more devastating than Washington's irrational immigration policy that fails to control the border.

During just the past four years, enough people to fill a city the size of Oakland [California] have illegally crossed the border into California. In Los Angeles alone, undocumented aliens and their children total nearly a million people. That's a city of illegal immigrants almost the size of San Diego.

I don't fault people trying to find a better life in our nation. In fact, it's hard not to admire their courage and determination. America is a nation of immigrants—three of my own grandparents were immigrants to America. They came for the same reason anyone comes—to build a better future. They brought their hopes and dreams, and the nation benefited from them and millions like them. But there's a limit to how quickly and

Pete Wilson, "Don't Give Me Your Tired, Your Poor . . . ," *The San Diego Union-Tribune*, January 9, 1994. Reprinted with permission.

how many immigrants we can assimilate at once.

If we ignore this flood of illegal immigration, we'll erode the quality of life for all those who live here legally.

Our classrooms are already bursting, but by federal law they're open to anyone who can clandestinely slip across America's 2,000-mile border. Our public health care facilities are being swamped, but two-thirds of all babies born in Los Angeles public hospitals are born to parents who have illegally entered the United States. And the budgets for our parks, beaches, libraries, and public safety will continue to suffer while California spends billions to incarcerate enough illegal aliens to fill eight state prisons.

Two-thirds of all babies born in Los Angeles public hospitals are born to parents who have illegally entered the United States.

The proposals we've heard in recent months—strengthening the Border Patrol, imposing a toll on those who cross the border, deporting more undocumented felons from our prisons—all acknowledge the need for action.

But none of them deals with the incentives by which federal law and immigration policy encourage illegal immigration, and indeed reward those who succeed in violating U.S. law by entering the United States illegally.

A failure of will in Washington

We need wholesale reform. We need to strike at the root of the problem. And the root of the problem lies not on our border, but in policies devised 3,000 miles to the east in our nation's capital.

The law is clear that the federal government alone has responsibility—for devising and implementing immigration law and policy. The immigration crisis facing America is the result of a failure of will in Washington.

Federal failure to deal with the problem is taking jobs from legal residents—many of them minorities—and killing the American dreams for those who suffer wage and job losses in California and every other state on our southern border.

That's why we must return reason and fairness to America's immigration laws.

The federal government has failed miserably at controlling the border. Crossing America's southern border is easier than crossing Prospect Street in La Jolla [California]. Millions have done it, and millions more will if we don't take action.

I've already urged President Clinton to seek assistance from the Mexican government to help stop the flood of illegal immigrants on the Mexican side of our border. But controlling the border isn't enough. In fact, there's little point in even having a Border Patrol if we're going to continue to reward those who successfully violate U.S. law and enter our country illegally.

Today, the federal government forces the states to give health care, education and other benefits to individuals who are in our country illegally. These mandated services to illegal immigrants and their children are costing California taxpayers $3.6 billion a year.

Because Washington forces us to fund these services for illegal immigrants, it means we have to cut $3.6 billion worth of health care, education and other services that are needed by, and would otherwise be available for, legal residents of California.

California has initiated an innovative program of preventive services for children in health care, mental health care and preschool, but funding for these programs is being siphoned off to programs for illegal immigrants mandated by the feds.

We're forced to cut aid for the needy elderly, blind and disabled who legally reside in California, because Washington mandates that we spend more than three-quarters of a billion dollars a year on emergency medical services for illegal aliens and more than a billion dollars a year to educate illegal aliens in our schools.

Services to illegal immigrants and their children are costing California taxpayers $3.6 billion a year.

Saving just the $1.7 billion we spend educating illegal immigrants in California schools would allow us to put a new computer on every fifth grader's school desk; provide pre-school services to tens of thousands of four-year-olds; expand Healthy Start Centers [facilities that provide health and social services to predominately low-income students] to hundreds of new sites, *and* provide more than 12 million hours of tutorial and mentoring services to at-risk youth.

Depriving legal California residents of these services is wrong. So I've urged Congress to repeal the federal mandates that require states to provide health care, education, and other benefits to illegal immigrants.

If the members of Congress had as much guts as most illegal immigrants—the guts to tell the truth—they'd admit that they are not only welching on their obligation but insisting that California and other states provide benefits to illegal immigrants even when it means denial of needed services to our legal residents.

The president and Congress should pay for these mandates as long as they require the states to provide them. And we're going to demand that they do meet that obligation and pay California the money they owe us.

Congress should then create a tamper-proof legal resident eligibility card and require it of everyone seeking government benefits.

Amend the Constitution

Finally, we must fundamentally rethink the very foundation of our immigration laws. The Constitution has been interpreted as granting citizenship to every child born in the United States, even the children of illegal aliens. Some illegals come to our country simply to have a child born on U.S. soil who can then gain American citizenship. That, of course, renders the child eligible for a host of public benefits. Just since 1988, the number of children of illegal aliens on our state's welfare rolls has grown more than four-fold.

It's time to amend the Constitution so that citizenship belongs only to the children of legal residents of the United States.

President Clinton did not create the grave problem of illegal immigration, he inherited it. But this exclusively federal responsibility now belongs to him and to Congress.

They must move without delay to enact these critical reforms to our nation's immigration laws. There is no time to waste, because the problem grows every day, swelled by the thousands of illegal aliens who slip across the border every night.

It's endangering the jobs we need to rebuild California's economy and the safety of too many California neighborhoods. And those most endangered in both ways are ironically the legal residents of the same ethnic groups.

We need immigration reform and we need it now.

5

Government Policies Should Be Reformed to Curb Asylum Abuse

Doris Meissner

Doris Meissner is the commissioner of the U.S. Immigration and Naturalization Service, the branch of the Department of Justice that oversees the nation's immigration laws and policies. She was previously a senior associate at the Carnegie Endowment for International Peace, a Washington, D.C., foreign policy think tank, where she directed its program on immigration and U.S. foreign policy.

Events of 1993 revealed the potential for immigrants to abuse the U.S. asylum system. Reforms instituted by the Immigration and Naturalization Service (INS) will enable officials to protect legitimate refugees (those fleeing persecution) while keeping out those who have no genuine need for asylum. Reforms include weeding out false asylum claims, expanding resources, and streamlining the asylum process.

In a way, the relocation of this [immigration asylum] office [in Arlington, Virginia] symbolizes the very phenomenon that makes this office and the whole Asylum Program necessary. The old place wasn't quite right for us, so we moved to a place that we liked better. That's really what people all over the world are doing more and more. They are leaving the places they were born in, and they are looking for places they can live in either more comfortably or more safely.

Now, no one leaves their homeland permanently seeking a new life elsewhere for easy or frivolous reasons. It's a heart-wrenching, often traumatic, decision. The problem is that there really is too much trauma, too much hardship, for too many people in today's world, and it forces governments, in the places where refuge is sought, to make an immigration policy distinction between true refugees fleeing persecution and others.

This distinction is still relatively new, formalized into U.S. law only with the passage of the Refugee Act of 1980 [which defined a refugee as someone with "a well founded fear of persecution on account of race, religion, nationality, membership in a particular social group, or political

From Doris Meissner's remarks at a press conference held for the official reopening of the Arlington, Virginia, Immigration Asylum Office of the Immigration and Naturalization Service, February 9, 1994.

opinions"]. It follows the principle that governments have not only the right, but the obligation to select who may come to their territories.

Asylum processing turns this orderly selection by governments around because the people choose the countries rather than the countries choosing the people. Thus, asylum processing becomes controversial for many, and can serve as an avenue for abuse for people with no other way of staying here.

In recent years, people purposefully seeking asylum are coming here in record numbers, many legitimately, yet some others ferried by smugglers and using false documents. Unfortunately, those that abuse the system have captured public attention. It really came to a head in 1993 because of the perceived linkage between asylum and events such as the World Trade Center bombing [on February 26, 1993], the shooting at the CIA [on January 25, 1993], and the Chinese smuggling ships [caught bringing illegal immigrants to the U.S. in 1993].

Such negative perceptions of asylum-seekers are insidious. They strain our traditional welcome of the oppressed. They cloud our judgment concerning the reasons that people seek refuge here.

Now, it's true that some use the asylum system as a means simply to get a work permit, but many others come here literally to stay alive. The ambiguity makes it very difficult not only to sort out who should stay and who should go back, but also to maintain support for the adjudication system that enables us to make the choice.

Governments have not only the right, but the obligation to select who may come to their territories.

That is why we are proposing a series of reforms that will preserve fundamental legal protection afforded to legitimate asylum seekers, while addressing the problems of asylum abuse.

The reforms are predicated on the idea that the American people do not want to close the door on those who are persecuted, but they are impatient with people who appear to be taking advantage of a process they don't really need or deserve.

In response to President Clinton's Immigration Initiatives announced last summer [1993], the Immigration Service and the Department of Justice have developed a plan for comprehensive reform. This plan has been followed by an announcement the week of January 24, 1994, of the resources that are required to implement the plan.

The reform plan focuses mainly on the affirmative Asylum Program. That is the program which deals with individuals who have already entered the United States and filed a claim for asylum.

In drafting our plan, we worked very closely with many individuals in this room, and I want to say again that we are enormously grateful for the responsiveness from the nongovernmental community, and the spirit of cooperation that we enjoyed in developing our proposals.

Key principles

Our proposals are guided by several key principles. First, asylum adjudications must be fair and timely, identifying bona fide refugees quickly so that they can be offered protection quickly.

Secondly, asylum adjudications must keep pace with receipts in order to deter abuses and preserve the integrity of the process.

Thirdly, adjudicators must receive specialized training and have access to up-to-date information about world conditions in response to increasingly complex reasons that lead people to migrate.

Finally, the system must be able to deport or require the departure of denied applicants promptly, at the end of the process.

Our reform plan combines regulatory and administrative changes to build a timely decision system. The regulatory proposal will be published in the Federal Register shortly.

I'd like to go over the key elements with you now, and then, at the conclusion of this program [the opening ceremony for the Arlington, Virginia, Immigration Asylum Office], I'm pleased to open up the floor for questions.

Four basic elements

There are four basic elements to the asylum reform that we are proposing. First of all, keeping out spurious asylum claims; secondly, keeping up with newly filed applications; thirdly, streamlining the asylum processing procedures; and, finally, addressing the backlogs of applications.

First, spurious claims. Tomorrow [February 10, 1994], we will begin to return applications when the evidence that is submitted either does not fully establish eligibility for the requested benefit, or raises underlying questions regarding eligibility. And we will ask the applicants in these cases for more specific information.

At the same time, some of our District and Asylum Offices are forming Asylum Abuse Task Forces, to bring enforcement actions, legal sanctions, and criminal prosecutions, where they are warranted, against the preparers of abusive claims.

Second, to keep up with newly filed applications, we are, as Gregg Beyer explained [in previous remarks], doubling the number of Asylum Officers from 150 to 334, by the end of this year [1994]. We are relocating or expanding six Asylum Offices in the same way as we have with this one, to accommodate the increased staff, and we are adding an eighth office in the New York area.

Thirdly, to streamline asylum processing and to fully implement the Asylum Reform Plan, we will seek some amendments to the law, we will promulgate new regulations, and we will seek increases in productivity through automation and through simplified procedures.

Finally, to address backlogs, once we have the staff increases and the processing reforms in place, we will become current with receipts, and then begin to work off the backlog of cases.

In closing, let me emphasize that reform can be accomplished without changing the purpose and the scope of U.S. and international asylum law. Under these reforms, anyone, from anywhere, at any time, regardless of entry or immigration status, may still apply for asylum in the United States, and not be returned to any place where he or she fears prosecution on account of race, religion, nationality, membership in a particular social group, or political opinion.

Generous protection for genuine refugees remains our goal. At the same time, these reforms restore needed balance to the process.

6

Immigration Should Be Suspended to Preserve the Nation

Pat Buchanan

Pat Buchanan is a nationally syndicated columnist.

Immigration is altering the racial composition of America; by 2050, whites may be near a minority. Consequently, American society is becoming increasingly divided along racial lines. The resulting ethnic tensions could cause the breakup of the United States in a manner similar to that of such multinational states as Czechoslovakia and Yugoslavia. America needs a ten-year "time out" on immigration to allow recent immigrants to assimilate.

If our prime minister believes that 50 years hence, "spinsters will still be cycling to Communion on Sunday morning," he had best think again. Rather, "the muezzin will be calling Allah's faithful to the high street mosque" for Friday prayers.

Thus did the grandson of Winston Churchill [in May 1993] call for a halt to the "relentless flow of immigrants" into Great Britain.

A volley of protest followed. "The *Times* of London chastised him for . . . a 'tasteless outburst,'" reports the *New York Times*. "(A) leading Labor Party politician described his remarks as 'putrid and racist.' Michael Howard, the Home Secretary, archly denounced what he described as 'any intervention which could have the effect of damaging race relations.'. . . Downing Street said Prime Minister John Major agreed with Mr. Howard."

But, on this issue, Churchill speaks for Europe and its growing concern over the swelling tide of immigration from the East and the Third World, and the impact on the fate and future of the West.

For Churchill's remark came just days before France's interior minister called for "zero immigration," and only days after Germany voted to amend its asylum law. Churchill spoke the same weekend a neo-Nazi teenager was charged with arson-murder in that firebombing in Solingen [Germany] that took the lives of five Turkish girls and women. The riots triggered by that atrocity left Solingen's town center gutted. All over Eu-

Pat Buchanan, "America Needs a 'Time Out' on Immigration," *Conservative Chronicle*, June 16, 1993. Reprinted by permission: Tribune Media Services.

rope the doors to the East and South are being shut.

Before condemning Germany for restricting asylum seekers, we ought to remember: Germany is smaller than Oregon and Washington combined, yet is home to almost 80 million people, among them 1.8 million Turks. Still, 167,000 new immigrants arrived in the first four months of 1993. (How would Oregon and Washington react to 500,000 immigrants this year?) Moreover, Germany has accepted more Bosnian refugees than all other nations combined.

To their credit, the Germans have coddled neither the neo-Nazi skinheads, nor the Turkish and leftist vandals—as some Americans did after our [1992] L.A. riots that made Solingen look like a panty raid.

But Germany today could be America tomorrow, if we do not address the twin issues of immigration and assimilation.

Brazil of North America

Consider the change in our own country in four decades. In 1950, America was a land of 150 million, 90 percent of European stock. Today the U.S. population is 250 million—about 75 percent white, 12 percent black, 9 percent Hispanic, and the balance largely Asian-American.

By 2050, according to the Census Bureau, whites may be near a minority in an America of 81 million Hispanics, 62 million blacks and 41 million Asians. By the middle of the next century, the United States will have become a veritable Brazil of North America.

If the future character of America is not to be decided by our own paralysis, Americans must stop being intimidated by charges of "racist," "nativist" and "xenophobe"—and we must begin to address the hard issues of race, culture and national unity.

Already, California faces yearly fiscal crises due to the soaring cost of services for illegal aliens, perhaps a million of whom walk into the United States every year from Mexico.

And the great American Melting Pot is not melting, as once it did. After decades of heroic effort to integrate blacks more fully into American society, our failures remain as conspicuous as our successes. Racial tension is rising. In the L.A. riots, not only were whites the victims of attempted lynchings, Koreatown was pillaged by blacks and Hispanics. Many of the latter were illegals, as four in ten felonies in San Diego county are the work of illegals.

The great American Melting Pot is not melting, as once it did.

While white-on-black crime has become relatively rare (white criminals choose black victims only 2 percent of the time) black criminals now choose white victims, in rapes and muggings, 50 percent of the time.

And demands are growing that our heritage of individual rights be superseded by a new system of racial entitlements. Quotas are routine in government and private business. On college campuses, there are new demands for all-black dorms and all-black cultural centers; blacks, whites, Hispanics and Asians tend to congregate, more and more, only with each other.

Supporters of open immigration contend that Hispanic, Asian and

Arab immigrants often bring with them the same strong family ties, respect for authority, and work ethic Americans have always cherished and celebrated.

Undeniably true. But it is equally true that many Third World immigrants are living off public services, and many are going into crime. It is also true that America's generous asylum laws are being abused. The man who allegedly murdered the CIA workers in McLean, Virginia [in January 1993], the men arrested for the World Trade Center bombing [in February 1993], were supposedly fleeing persecution abroad.

America needs to take what some have called a "time out" on immigration: a closing of our southern frontier to invading illegals, by troops if necessary, a toughening of our asylum laws, a cutback on legal immigration to spouses and minor children of those already here.

Looking back down the 20th century, we see that all the great multinational empires have fallen apart. Now, the multinational states—Canada, Czechoslovakia, India, Russia, Yugoslavia, South Africa, Ethiopia—are breaking apart. Are we immune to all this?

After a quarter century of wide-open immigration, we need at least a decade to assimilate the tens of millions who have come in. Else, Russia's fate in the '90s may be America's in the new century.

7

Immigration Should Be Reduced to Strengthen U.S. Competitiveness

Lawrence E. Harrison

Lawrence E. Harrison has directed development programs for the U.S. Agency for International Development, a government office that provides assistance to underdeveloped countries. He is the author of Underdevelopment Is a State of Mind: The Latin American Case *and* Who Prospers? How Cultural Values Shape Economic and Political Success.

Since the end of World War II, large numbers of unskilled workers have been allowed to immigrate to the United States. Due to the resulting abundance of cheap labor, American industries have relied on labor-intensive means of production and have failed to advance technologically. Consequently, the economic competitiveness of the United States relative to other developed countries is poor. In order to improve America's economic strength, immigration should be limited to a small number of skilled workers.

High levels of immigration, legal and illegal, have not produced the positive economic results that growth-minded advocates have expected. For four decades, we have accepted vastly more immigrants than any other advanced country. Yet despite the big head start the U.S. economy enjoyed after World War II, our average performance measured over the last 40 years has been among the worst of the developed nations, roughly comparable to Britain's. Many other factors explain the decline of U.S. competitiveness, but the low-skill immigration of recent decades has surely not been helpful, except to labor-intensive businesses that have profited from the supply of cheap labor—leaving the community at large to pick up the social costs.

Of course, many proponents of large-scale immigration are motivated by humanitarian rather than economic concerns, the potentially adverse impact on American citizens notwithstanding. I'm reminded of a comment made about her own country by the Australian sociologist Katherine Betts in her book *Ideology and Immigration*: "Humanitarianism became

Lawrence E. Harrison, "Huddled Masses, Unskilled Labor," *The Washington Post National Weekly Edition*, January 20-26, 1992. Reprinted with permission.

the chief goal of immigration for some people and immigration itself came to be seen as a form of international aid. . . . The relatively poor in this country pay a disproportionate share of the cost of the conscience of the rich."

In *The Competitive Advantage of Nations*, Harvard economist Michael E. Porter stresses the contribution skilled immigrants can make to "the principal economic goal of a nation—a high and rising standard of living." But he goes on to note that large-scale immigration of the unskilled may retard the process.

During the past 40 years, America outpaced all other developed countries in population growth. Immigration, legal and illegal, has been a major contributor to that growth. Since 1950, 20 million people have immigrated legally. No one knows how many have entered illegally. Estimates range from 5 million to 8 million. In the wake of liberalizing legislation in 1990, upwards of 1 million immigrants are now entering annually.

Over this period, U.S. immigration policy has emphasized political concerns—e.g., Cuba, Vietnam—and family relationships, not skills, and has done little to curb the vast flow of illegal immigrants. The result, as George Borjas concludes in *Friends or Strangers*, has been that "the skill composition of the immigrant flow has deteriorated significantly in the past two or three decades."

The large majority of both legal and illegal newcomers will arrive with few skills.

The loss of competitive advantage of many U.S. products in recent decades is importantly the consequence of the slow growth of labor productivity. That is partly the result of low levels of U.S. research, development and investment compared with our principal competitors, Japan and Germany. But it is also the consequence of a labor force relatively unskilled by comparison with Japan's and Germany's, a labor force whose real income has been declining while the incomes of Japanese and German workers have been increasing. American wages are no longer the highest in the world.

In fact, the United States now emphasizes relatively cheap labor—a good part of it available because of immigration—much as Third World countries do. Aside from the retreat from the objective of a rising standard of living implicit in it, cheap labor encourages investors to use labor-intensive means of production, and that means slow or no technological advance and further slippage in our competitive position. The resulting slow overall growth of the economy has meant lower federal, state and local revenues. Porter notes, "The ability to compete despite paying higher wages would seem to represent a far more desirable national target."

I want to repeat that immigration is but one of several causes of our economic malaise. But it is not an insignificant one.

Immigrants compete with citizens

Some researchers, Borjas among them, have concluded that immigrants—legal or illegal—do not compete with native-born Americans, although they do compete with other immigrants, including many who have been here long enough to become citizens. More recent studies, including those of Rice University's Don Huddle, conclude that immigrants do indeed compete with natives, especially when unemployment is relatively high.

Immigration proponents argue that immigrants—particularly illegal immigrants—accept wages and working conditions that citizens, even poor citizens, wouldn't. Even accepting that argument, the obvious implication is that employers would have to pay more and provide better working conditions if there were not an ample supply of immigrants. But, in fact, there are cases of displacement, for example in Los Angeles, where building maintenance workers, mostly black, have been displaced by immigrants, mostly Mexican. Moreover, immigrants may well compete with poorer citizens for low-cost housing—which means higher rentals—and public services, including education.

It is both sensible and moral to base our policies primarily on the needs of our own society.

Several researchers, for example, the Urban Institute's Thomas Muller and Thomas Espenshade, have also studied the extent to which immigrants are a burden on public budgets, e.g., welfare, social services, subsidized housing, education. Two principal conclusions emerge: 1) what most immigrants pay in taxes does not cover the costs of the services they receive, particularly when education is included; and 2) the downward trend in immigrant skills has been accompanied by an upward trend in their use of public assistance.

The problem of refugee/immigrant demand for services has been particularly acute in Massachusetts, where the Dukakis administration adopted a policy of insuring the availability of all state services to refugees, and both the state and city of Boston provided many services to immigrants without reference to the legality of their status.

Massachusetts consequently became a magnet for immigrants. Between 1980 and 1990, the Hispanic population more than doubled to 288,000, while the Asian population almost tripled to 143,000. The treatment of immigrants did not become a really hot issue until the sharp downturn in the state's economy and the resulting budget crisis. Now there can be no question that immigrants compete for drastically reduced public services with needy citizens.

Immigration policy should reflect U.S. needs

We are a society imbued with Emma Lazarus's words on the Statue of Liberty: "Give me your tired, your poor, your huddled masses yearning to breathe free." When the statue was dedicated 105 years ago, some 60 million people lived in the United States. The frontier was still open, and an open immigration policy clearly suited our needs. Today, our population is more than four times greater, the frontier is long gone and population growth is a principal contributor to the pressure on the environment that so preoccupies us.

Congress passed a law in 1990 that increases legal immigration by 40 percent. Congress took this action in the face of repeated polls showing an overwhelming majority of Americans—including 74 percent of Hispanic Americans and 78 percent of black Americans in a 1990 Roper survey—oppose increased immigration.

Despite new emphasis on skills in the 1990 legislation, more than 70 percent of legal newcomers will enter because they are related to naturalized citizens, resident aliens and former illegal immigrants who qualified for the amnesty provisions of the 1986 immigration act. The large majority of both legal and illegal newcomers will arrive with few skills.

The Haitian boat people are a case in point. Almost all have risked their lives in leaky vessels to reach the United States. Although some of the earlier boat people were refugees from François Duvalier's political persecution, that the flow increased over the previous year's during the eight months when President Jean-Bertrand Aristide, the landslide populist winner of the 1990 elections, was in office, demonstrates that most seek economic opportunity and social services that vastly exceed what their homeland offers.

A 1985 study of recent Haitian immigrants in Florida revealed the following: Average years of education were 4.6; 5 percent were high school graduates; 82 percent had limited or no English; 93 percent had limited or no knowledge of the United States; 63 percent were unemployed; 29 percent were receiving welfare aid.

Although there must always be room in our immigration policies for dealing with cases of special hardship, in a world in which hundreds of millions of people would gladly come to our shores, choices must be made. No immigration policy can remedy the failures of other nations to meet the needs of their poor, so it is both sensible and moral to base our policies primarily on the needs of our own society, particularly economic revival and raising the standard of living of our poorer citizens. That means a significant reduction in legal immigration, redoubled programs to control illegal immigration and an upgrading of the skills of those immigrants we accept. These measures won't solve America's economic problems, but they will certainly help.

8

Immigration Should Be Restricted for Environmental Reasons

Leon F. Bouvier

Leon F. Bouvier is an adjunct professor of demography at Tulane University School of Public Health in New Orleans, Louisiana. He has served as a demographic adviser to Congress and as vice president of the Population Reference Bureau, a nonprofit organization that studies population trends. He is the author of Immigration and Social Diversity *and* Peaceful Invasions: Immigration and Changing America.

Due largely to immigration, U.S. population is projected to grow from 254 million in 1990 to 388 million to 454 million in 2050. This growth in America's population will exacerbate the following national and world environmental problems: increased global warming, air pollution, and waste production; decreased food production and water supplies; the destruction of the wetlands and infrastructure. Immigration levels should be reduced to prevent further environmental destruction.

Virtually all discussions in Congress about legal immigration center on questions of *who* this nation should permit to immigrate so as to benefit the nation's labor force. The 1990 [Immigration Act] legislation, for example, concerned itself with the occupational characteristics as well as the country of origin of potential immigrants. The larger question, of *how many* immigrants are appropriate, was not discussed. Yet, as a result of this legislation, the United States population in 2050 will be about 35 million larger than it would be if such legislation were not passed. This failure to take population growth into account is unfortunate, because the number of immigrants the United States admits is not only a major determinant of future United States population size, but also has significant ramifications for environmental protection.

[As of 1990, about 254 million people live in the United States.] If current demographic trends are maintained, there will be 388 million Americans in the year 2050. With slight increases in fertility and immigration, there could be 454 million Americans in the year 2050. Looking farther into the future, the range of possibilities becomes even more dramatic: the same scenario that produces 454 million Americans in 2050 leads to 900 million Americans by 2120. Demographers Ahlburg and Vaupel foresee a possible population of 811 million by 2080.

> A U.S. population of 800 million may seem incredible, but the annual average growth rate that produces it runs at only 1.3 percent per year. This is the same as the average annual growth rate that has prevailed in the United States over the last half-century and not too much above the 1 percent average annual growth rate of the last decade.[1]

In other words, the United States could have more people in 100 years than India has today. This is not a welcome prospect.

Public policy and population growth

Public policy in the United States influences fertility in subtle and not-so-subtle ways. State and federal governments fund (or don't fund) family planning clinics; restrict (or don't restrict) the availability of abortion; provide (or don't provide) sex education and population education. In many diverse ways, our national and state governments and the culture in general influence family size decisions. But these decisions remain— and should remain—those of individuals alone. Changes in life expectancy also affect the size of the population. But all agree that life expectancy should be increased for all Americans. Immigration remains the one aspect of domestic population growth that is—in theory at least—regulated by the federal government in the national interest.

The United States could have more people in 100 years than India has today.

With fertility at late 1980 levels (1.8 births per woman) and net immigration reduced to 350,000, stabilization could be achieved by the middle of the next century at about 316 million; or, with increased fertility and immigration, the United States could be on a course toward a virtually unimaginable one billion Americans.

Thus, immigration policy is a far-reaching means to influence population growth. Goals for U.S. population size should be an essential part of every discussion of immigration policy.

U.S. population growth and the environment

Environmental protection is a matter of widespread concern in the United States and throughout the world. Millions of Americans participated in Earth Day celebrations in spring of 1990. Some three-quarters of Americans consider themselves environmentalists as measured by polls, and membership in environmental groups has been rising dramatically. The political importance of environmental issues can be seen in the extent to which elected officials (and those campaigning for public office) make the claim to be solidly for the environment. Even President George Bush proclaims himself to be the "environment president."

Although *domestic* population growth has been far from the public eye since the early 1970s, environmental groups (including the Sierra Club and Population-Environment-Balance for example) have long believed that human population growth is harmful to the environment, and that population stabilization is essential in the long run if environmental goals are to be achieved and maintained.

Global climate change

The drought of 1988, together with the unseasonably warm winter of 1989, made all Americans aware that this warming trend was a possible harbinger of the dreaded "greenhouse effect." Many respected scientists are warning that the greenhouse effect could cause unprecedented disruption to the global environment.

Many gases emitted into the earth's atmosphere (including carbon dioxide, methane, chlorofluorocarbons, and nitrous oxide) are known to trap heat. The concentration of these "greenhouse gases" will continue to increase until significant changes are made in energy use. It is estimated that the earth is already committed to an average temperature increase of 3.5–9 degrees Fahrenheit (2–5 degrees Centigrade) before a new equilibrium is achieved. This is an increase without precedent in recorded history.

In order to slow the rate of build-up of greenhouse gases, far-reaching measures must be adopted. Those recommended by the Sierra Club include: (1) a ban on the production and releases of chlorofluorocarbons, which not only contribute to the greenhouse effect but are also the chief culprits in the destruction of the stratospheric ozone layer; (2) a decrease in the use of coal and increase in the energy conservation and the use of renewable energy sources; (3) a halt to the destruction of forest ecosystems and a major program of reforestation; (4) a greatly increased effort to reduce the rate of population growth in each country of the world, with the eventual goal of a stabilized world population size.

Although population growth is more rapid in developing nations, per capita energy use in the United States is so large that even a small rate increase of population growth in the United States results in large increases in energy use—and hence, production of greenhouse gases.

Not only would the United States benefit directly from a stabilization of its own population, but people throughout the world would benefit through reduced United States production of greenhouse gases.

Food production

The United States has long been a food exporting nation. Given the demands of many rapidly growing nations of the Third World and parts of Eastern Europe, this is very fortunate. However, with increasing population and growing individual consumption by Americans, surpluses in food production are dwindling rapidly.

In 1972, USDA [United States Department of Agriculture] experts concluded that:

> American agriculture appears capable . . . of meeting the challenges of the year 2000. Even under the most demanding assumptions about food and constraints on technology, food and fiber needs could be met without great difficulty, but would require some increase in prices.... If this analysis were continued out to the year 2020, the cost of bringing additional farmland into production could possibly increase food prices substantially.[2]

More recently entomologist David Pimentel testified before the Select Commission on Immigration and Refugee Policy that if soil erosion can be stopped and if the availability of energy at today's relative prices is unchanged, the United States could increase productivity (and thus production) by 25 to 30 percent over the next 50 years.[3]

Goals for U.S. population size should be an essential part of every discussion of immigration policy.

The United States population will grow by over 35 percent between 1990 and 2040. If this rate is not reduced, either Americans will be eating less well or American farmers will be exporting far fewer food products. To be sure, new agronomy methods may be discovered which will increase productivity beyond Pimentel's estimates. However, this only postpones the inevitable. If the United States population keeps growing, sooner or later food production will be insufficient for export.

Not only will this be harmful for the countries in dire need of food imports, it will also pose problems for the United States trade deficit where food exports help keep that deficit lower than it otherwise would be.

Water supply

Water shortage is a large and growing problem in some parts of the nation. This is not a new problem. In 1972, in a report prepared for the Commission on Population Growth and the American Future, Ronald Ridker concluded,

> Growth in population and economic activities during the next half century will force upon us significant expenditures for treatment and storage facilities [of water]; moreover, for a growing number of regions, such investments will eventually prove inadequate. When one takes a region-by-region look at the situation, it becomes clear that the scope for redistribution of water, activities, and people is more limited and difficult to achieve than it might appear at first glance.[4]

Some eighteen years later the problem of adequate water supply remains.[5] Average per capita withdrawal in the United States increased 22 percent between 1970 and 1980. This was less than the 37 percent increase of the previous ten years, but still roughly twice the rate of population growth. In 1985, average water withdrawal by Americans amounted to 1,950 gallons per person, of which 450 gallons were consumed. Americans use about three times as much water per capita as do the Japanese.[6]

Furthermore, water supply is not evenly distributed, with the west receiving 30 percent of the fresh water runoff but accounting for 80 percent of the consumption. In California, these problems are compounded by rapid population growth. A report by the National Academy of Sciences says that in order to accommodate the needs of the burgeoning population in California more water will have to be shipped in from someplace else. And that someplace else will be harder, if not impossible, to find.[7]

Regarding water quality, the 1987 Council of State Governments report concludes:

> For the first time we are confronted with water quality problems everywhere. Every state is experiencing contaminated groundwater supplies, unsafe drinking water, and higher costs for maintaining a

supply of water to meet growing demand. These problems are a result of modern society and will become more severe with the *growth of population* and the expansion of the man-made environment.[8] (emphasis added)

Air quality

There is sufficient air for all of us to breathe. However, it does not take a doomsayer to be alarmed at the quality of that air that all of us breathe. About 90 percent of the air pollutants in the United States can be attributed to the burning of fossil fuels. Half of all the air pollutants come from motor vehicles and another 28 percent come from power and industrial plants. Air quality improved during the 1970s in large part due to the passage of the Clean Air Acts of 1970 and 1977. Between 1982 and 1985, however, ambient levels of major pollutants other than lead either remained the same or climbed slightly. These increases are the result of Reagan administration cutbacks in enforcement of air pollution control regulations.

They are also the result of growth. Clearly, clean air cannot be achieved without strong pollution controls on individual automobiles and on emissions from factories. Yet, as many metropolitan areas have discovered, the sheer amount of growth, by putting more automobiles on the road, can erode gains achieved at great cost through emission controls. Fortunately, a new Clean Air Act was passed in late 1990. However, in order to be successful, a Clean Air Act must also incorporate a plan for population stabilization, not only for the nation as a whole, but also for specific areas with severe air quality problems.

Waste disposal

Landfills everywhere are nearing capacity and public opinion opposes "imported waste." All Americans remember the 1988 two-month odyssey of the infamous Islip, Long Island, garbage barge. During that barge's travel it was refused permission to unload its cargo by six states and three countries. Ultimately that cargo was burned in a Brooklyn incinerator. In 1990, Indiana objected strenuously to continued garbage disposal in that state by New Jersey. These episodes illustrate the enormous sewage and waste disposal problems Americans are facing. The United States produces 160 million tons of municipal solid waste per year, nearly 3.5 pounds per day for every man, woman, and child in the nation. With expected increases in population as well as in consumption, the 200 million ton per year mark will soon be reached. Even without any increases in consumption, that mark will be reached within 20 years.

Problems are greater in large metropolitan areas. Southern California, for example, has already reached its limits for burying garbage: the landfills are full. Sewage problems are equally severe.

> Spills of raw sewage into the ocean off Southern California are becoming commonplace. Fish found in the Santa Monica Bay are not edible due to diseases and contamination. The city of Los Angeles processes most of its sewage at the Hyperion Sewage Treatment plant which is unable to keep up with demands caused by increased population. Because of this, 800 million gallons of only minimally treated sewage spews into the ocean every day.[9]

On the Atlantic, similar problems are emerging as noted by the garbage found on New Jersey shores and elsewhere in recent summers.

The proportion of materials recycled can certainly be greatly improved and waste production can be reduced. Yet even if per capita production of wastes is halved, should the population double, the nation will be even worse off than when it started, because waste production will be back at the same level, with the easy waste-reduction steps already having been taken.

Wetlands

Far too little attention is being paid to the staggering loss of inland wetlands throughout the United States. "Located away from ocean tides, these are the bogs and swamps that act as nature's sponges. They soak up pollutants, provide breeding grounds and habitat for wildlife including migratory fowl. Without these humble swamps, floods become a far greater menace."[10]

Because choice lands are already developed, draining the nation's inland wetlands to make way for development is increasing despite federal and state laws designed to protect these diminishing wetlands. Over half of the nation's wetlands have been destroyed and at least an additional 300,000 acres are destroyed every year—all for housing and commercial development. Unfortunately, the Bush administration's recent redefinition of "wetlands" will exacerbate the problem.

Infrastructure

The infrastructure problems facing the United States are growing. Roads, bridges, water systems, railroads and mass transit are all deteriorating. According to the Report of the National Governors' Association 1989 meeting, the price to bring America's transportation infrastructure into reasonable condition within the next 20 years is estimated to range from $1 trillion to $3 trillion, requiring annual outlays in the range of $50 billion to $150 billion.[11] Roads and bridges are the biggest problems. Over 200,000 miles of the nation's roads are in "poor" or "very poor" shape, and another million miles are rated only "fair." Of the nation's 575,000 highway bridges, 42 percent are structurally deficient or functionally obsolete. In some regions of the country, many bridges have already deteriorated to the point of being safety hazards for the public.

Over the last two decades, traffic has grown five times faster than highway capacity. In the next two decades, congestion is projected to become five times worse. In California, transportation officials fear that it will be virtually impossible for enough new highway miles to be constructed to keep pace with population growth. Similar problems are noted in most of the nation's metropolitan areas as suburbs are extended farther and farther away from the central cities to accommodate the burgeoning population. The result is sprawl development, choked highways and massive traffic congestion. The average speed on Los Angeles freeways, already a very low 37 miles per hour, is projected to drop to 17 miles per hour by the year 2000.

The list of population-related infrastructure problems is almost endless. Consider the nation's crowded beaches and National Parks; consider its deteriorating water and sewage systems; consider its transit system, whether bus, plane or train. "Airports anticipate a 72 percent increase in passenger volume in this decade; by 1997, 33 major airports are expected to experience, cumulatively, 20,000 hours of delays annually."[12]

Population growth worsens each of these problems. All levels of government are struggling to catch up with the needs of growing numbers, and all too often fail to maintain the systems built in the past or to improve them for the future.

Consider too that the added 100 or 200 million Americans will not be equally distributed among the 50 states. Visualize more than 50 million people living in California, at least 25 million in Southern California, compared to 15 million today. Visualize 30 million people living in Texas; another 30 million in Florida, and yet another 25 million in New York, with more than half of them in the New York City metropolitan area. Without any movement to such underpopulated places as the Dakotas and Montana, such regional population concentrations are a distinct possibility if the United States population increases by 100 million or more over the next 60 years.

World population growth

World population increase is widely recognized as one of the most serious problems facing humankind. Scientist Norman Myers has called the 1990s "the most decisive decade in humankind's history," the "final window of opportunity" to come to grips with the world's population and environmental problems, and protect the habitability of the planet. Myers, in considering how much environmental destruction has already been made inevitable, examines an unusual hypothesis:

> Suppose that in the year 2000, humanity were to be eliminated from the face of the Earth. The in-built inertia of [biological] decline would by then be so great that species would continue to disappear in ever larger numbers, due to "delayed fall-out processes." The ecological injury already done would have triggered the irreversible unravelling of food webs, leading to domino-effect extinctions for many decades, even for a whole century.[13]

Imagine the environmental destruction associated with a world population of 10 or 15 billion!

The root of all these problems can be traced at least in part to the incredible rate of population growth on the planet. Just 150 years ago, world population reached one billion. Recently, the 5 billion mark was passed. In the last hour or so . . . 16,000 babies were born while about 6,000 people died. The world's population increased by 10,000 people.

In 1980, in his farewell message to the nation, President Jimmy Carter addressed the problems of population and the environment:

> There are real and growing dangers to our simple and most precious possessions; the air we breathe; the water we drink; and the land which sustains us. The rapid depletion of irreplaceable minerals, the erosion of topsoil, the destruction of beauty, the blight of pollution, the demand of increasing billions of people, all combine to create problems which are easy to observe and predict, but difficult to resolve. If we do not act, the world of the year 2000 will be much less able to sustain life than it is now. But there is no reason for despair. Acknowledging these realities is the first step in dealing with them. We can meet the resource problems of the world—water, food, minerals, farmlands, forests, overpopulation, pollution—if we tackle them with courage and foresight.

Unfortunately, President Carter's successors have not heeded his warnings. Concern about *world* population growth is widespread and not seriously questioned. However, a few widely quoted individuals have argued that, in effect, the United States is exempt from the principle that population stabilization is beneficial. They claim that growth is beneficial for the United States.

This is simply wrong. The United States does not need population increase beyond the 60 million increase that is virtually inevitable. Rather, every expansion of the number of Americans hurts the nation's ability to solve its environmental and other problems. Indeed, environmental scientists David and Marcia Pimentel argue that: "For the United States to be self-sustaining in solar energy, given our land, water, and biological resources, our population should be less than 100 million. . . . However, with a drastic reduction in standard of living, the current population level might be sustained."[14]

Because the average consumption of Americans far exceeds that of any other country, any increase in the number of Americans has a disproportionate negative effect. According to Norman Myers:

> The one billion people at the top of the pile generally do not feature high population rates, but such are their materialist life-styles—many of them, for instance, consume 100 times as much commercial energy as do most Bangladeshis, Ethiopians, and Bolivians—that in certain respects the additional 1.75 million Americans each year may well do as much damage to the biosphere as the 85 million additional Third Worlders.[15]

Large-scale immigration to the United States helps the few who migrate, but harms the billions who do not. In terms of global warming, waste production, energy use, and many other environmental concerns, citizens of the world can breathe easier when United States population stops increasing. It does not matter whether United States population increase comes from fertility or immigration—ending it helps protect both the world environment and the environment of the United States.

Large-scale immigration to the United States helps the few who migrate, but harms the billions who do not.

Furthermore it is quite possible that a portion of the very recent increase in fertility [to 2.0 births per woman in 1990] may reflect the changing ethnic proportions of the population. As long as these ethnic shares continue to grow, overall fertility will rise. As long as the fertility of minority groups surpasses that of the current majority population, the growing numbers in the minorities will raise the nation's overall fertility.

Let us assume that the current total fertility rates for the four principal ethnic groups in the United States are as follows: Anglo 1.8; Black 2.3; Hispanic 3.0; Asian and Others 2.3. While we cannot vouch for the accuracy of these figures, they are undoubtedly close to the eventual figures for 1990. Let us further assume that shifts in the ethnic composition of the population will be as follows. The Anglo share will fall from 76 percent in 1990 to 65 in 2020 and 54 in 2050 while that for Hispanics will rise from 9 percent to 15 and 22 percent, and others accordingly.

Given these assumptions, the total fertility rate would rise from 2.0 in 1990 to 2.1 in 2020 and 2.2 in 2050—without any actual increases in the fertility of any one ethnic group, but rather as a result of "shifting shares" in the overall population. Such "small" increases of 0.1 every thirty years may seem inconsequential. They are not. According to recent Census Bureau projections, the difference between fertility remaining constant at 1.8 and fertility gradually rising to 2.2 by 2050 (while holding mortality and migration constant) amounts to over 63 million by that year![16] A very slight increase in fertility yields massive increases in population size decades later. Given these numbers, it would appear that any end to population growth in the United States is nowhere in sight so long as immigration levels remain high.

Notes

1. Dennis A. Ahlburg and J.W. Vaupel, 1990. "Alternative Projections of the U.S. Population." *Demography* 27, no. 4: 645.

2. A. Barry Carr and David W. Culver, "Agriculture, Population and the Environment," in R. Ridker, ed., *Population, Resources and the Environment* (Commission on American Growth and the American Future, Washington: Government Printing Office, 1972), 193-94.

3. David Pimentel, testimony before the Select Commission on Immigration and Refugee Policy, 1980.

4. Ronald Ridker, *Resource and Environmental Consequences of Population Growth in the United States: A Summary* (Commission on American Growth and the American Future, Washington: GPO, 1972), 221.

5. Water withdrawal must be distinguished from water consumption. Withdrawal involves taking water from a groundwater or surface water source and transporting it to a place of use. Consumption occurs when water that has been withdrawn is not available for reuse in the area from which it is withdrawn. (G. Tyler Miller, *Resource Conservation and Management* [Belmont: Wadsworth Publishing Co., 1990], 185.)

6. Kenneth R. Sheets, "War Over Water: Crisis of the Eighties." *U.S. News & World Report*, 31 October 1983, 7.

7. As cited by Dawn Glesser Moore, testimony before the Subcommittee on Census and Population of the Committee on Post Office and Civil Service, U.S. House of Representatives, 12 April 1988, 3.

8. Kenneth Cole, "Clean Water: National Issue, Regional Concern," in *States' Summit '87: Issues and Choices for the 1990s*, Council of State Governments Annual Meeting, Boston, December 1987, 8.

9. Moore, testimony, 19.

10. Neal Peirce, "Breakthrough for Wetlands: EPA's Reilly Lobbies a Maryland Law," *The Virginian-Pilot*, 22 May 1989, A-7.

11. As cited in David Broder, "On the Roads Again: Governors in the Lead," *The Washington Post*, 8 August 1989,12.

12. George Will, "Congealed in Traffic," *The Washington Post*, 11 March 1990, B7.

13. Norman Myers, "People and Environment: The Watershed Decade," *People* (London) 17, no. 1 (1990): 17.

14. David Pimentel and Marcia Pimentel, "Land, Energy and Water: The Constraints Governing Ideal U.S. Population Size," *The NPG Forum* (1990): 5.

15. Myers, "People and Environment," 19.

16. U.S. Bureau of the Census, *Projections of the Population of the United States, by Age, Sex, and Race: 1988 to 2080*, 16.

9

The Roman Catholic Church's Position on Immigration Is Irresponsible

David Simcox

David Simcox, a Roman Catholic, was the first executive director of the Center for Immigration Studies (CIS), from 1985 to 1992.

Since World War II, the Roman Catholic Church has averred that the right of people to migrate is more significant than the right of nations to control their borders. American church leaders have consistently challenged the legitimacy of U.S. laws limiting immigration. These efforts have produced results inconsistent with church teachings. For example, encouraging emigration to America as a means to relieve suffering in poor countries has exacerbated poverty in the United States, while ignoring the drain of human resources from sending countries. The Catholic Church should weigh its charitable principles against the social, economic, and environmental concerns that impel government to restrict immigration.

> For which of you, intending to build a tower, sitteth not down first, and counteth the cost, whether he have sufficient to finish it? (Luke 14:28)

Do sovereign nations have the inherent right to limit immigration? Catholic teaching since World War II has moved from a qualified "yes" to a presumption of "no," with the moral legitimacy of the rare exception depending on the exigencies of the moment.

This shifting theology bespeaks the rapid evolution in the structure of the church, in Rome and in the United States; in the increasing size and mobility of world populations; and in the way the church sees itself and its mission in the world. The Vatican Council in the 1960s renewed emphasis on ecumenism, internationalism, the indivisibility of the human family, and social activism. Migration, in the process, became sacralized. Rather than a social process which nations must manage, mass migration is an expression of the divine plan, a providential, redeeming

David Simcox, "The Catholic Hierarchy and Immigration: Boundless Compassion, Limited Responsibility." Reprinted with permission from the Winter 1992/1993 issue of *The Social Contract*, a quarterly journal treating population, immigration, and resource concerns, 316½ E. Mitchell, Suite 4, Petoskey, MI 49770.

force for the realization of universal human solidarity.

The church's assertion of the primacy of the needs of individual migrants partakes of its concern for the value and dignity of human life everywhere which has shaped its teaching on contraception and abortion. The scriptural verse: "Love the stranger then, for you were strangers in the land of Egypt" (Deuteronomy 10: 18-19) is seen as summing up the "fundamental ethic of welcome, care, and solidarity towards every kind of immigrant" required of Christians.

The church vs. the nation-state

Pius XII, Christ's vicar (1939–1958) in a world beginning to experience explosive population growth and unprecedented mobility, became the first Pontiff to affirm an explicit, though conditional, "right" to migrate:

> Public authorities unjustly deny the rights of human persons if they block or impede emigration or immigration except where grave requirements of the common good, considered objectively, demand it (*Speeches*, 1959).

His successor, Pope John XXIII, also voiced the emerging doctrine of "just reasons" for immigration:

> Every human being has the right to freedom of movement and of residence within the confines of his own country; and, when there are just reasons for it, the right to emigrate to other countries and take up residence there (*Pacem in Terris*).

The right to emigrate was enshrined in the United Nations' Universal Declaration of Human Rights, which does not, however, contain any right of *immigration:*

> Article 13. (1) Everyone has the right to freedom of movement and residence within the borders of each state. (2) Everyone has the right to leave any country, including his own, and to return to his country

> Article 14. (1) Everyone has the right to seek and to enjoy in other countries asylum from persecution. (2) This right may not be invoked in the case of prosecutions genuinely arising from non-political crimes or from acts contrary to the purposes and principles of the United Nations.

The right to immigrate had been explicitly rejected by most nations [at the United Nations], including the United States. *Pacem in Terris* proclaims the promotion of the personal rights of all as the primary end of governments. This encyclical deplored the inadequacy of nation-states and the international system to realize the common good and the rights of individuals (Christiansen, 1988). Pope John implied a preference for world government, but prescribed neither structures nor roadmaps.

Pacem in Terris evokes the underlying historical tension between the Catholic church and the nation-state, with its concepts of geographically defined jurisdiction and obligations, exclusive sovereignty, and the supremacy of national interests. In the three decades since John XXIII, the church has become even more antagonistic toward national assertions of sovereignty, not only in the movement of peoples across borders, but in the international flow of trade, knowledge, culture and capital.

Pope Paul VI in 1967 affirmed more explicitly the right to migrate for economic betterment: "Every human being has the right to leave one's country of origin for various motives—and return to it as well—in order to seek better living conditions" (cited in Mahony, 1987).

World bishops, meeting at the Vatican in 1969, updated and codified the teachings on migration. The resulting document, *Instruction for the Pastoral Care of Peoples Who Migrate*, asserts the following rights (*Congregation of Bishops*, 1969):

• The right to a homeland.

• The right of people to emigrate, as individuals or as families, when a state, because of poverty and "great population" cannot meet their needs, or denies their basic dignity. Migrants' right to live together as a family is to be safeguarded. Only the "grave requirements of the common good, considered objectively," can justify abridgment of these rights.

• The right to keep one's native tongue and spiritual heritage.

Instructions from the Congregation of Bishops spelled out obligations and duties for the migrants themselves—obligations that are rarely mentioned now in debating the morality of immigration control:

• The prospective migrants' obligation to remember that they have the right and duty to contribute to the progress of their home community:

> Especially in underdeveloped areas where all resources must be put to urgent use, those men gravely endanger the public good who, particularly possessing mental powers or wealth, are enticed by greed and temptation to emigrate. The developed regions should not omit to consider this perversion of the common good of the less developed regions. Let them foster the preparation and return to the homeland of artisans and students, once they achieve ability in their fields.

• Governing authorities of sending states have the parallel duty to seek the creation of jobs in their own regions:

> We advocate in such cases the policy of bringing the work to the workers, wherever possible, rather than drafting workers to the scene of the work. In this way migrations will be the result, not of compulsion, but of free choice.

• Migrants themselves have the duty to accommodate themselves to the host country:

> Anyone who is going to encounter another people should have great esteem for their patrimony and their language and their customs. Therefore let immigrating people accommodate themselves willingly to a host community and hasten to learn its language, so that, if their residence there turns out to be long or even definitive, they may be able to be integrated more easily into their new society.

The Vatican and immigration

The Vatican's concern for immigrants' rights has been further elaborated under John Paul II. "Solidarity among all peoples" has become a central theme in the Vatican's approach to international relations, and to immigration in particular. Solidarity, as the Vatican describes it, is not a matter of compassion but justice, not a question of economics but ethics (*Final Document*, 1991). Echoing open-border economist Julian Simon and other influential cornucopian thinkers, the Vatican proclaims solidarity to be its own reward: "experience shows that when a nation has the courage to open its frontiers to immigration, it is rewarded by increased prosperity, a solid renewal of society and a vigorous drive towards new economic and human goals" (*Final Document*, 1991).

John Paul II has reaffirmed the immorality of immigration restrictions except where justified by "serious and well-founded reasons." He has not stated the conditions for legitimate restriction with a specificity helpful to earthly policymakers. In 1990 he told Italian auto workers:

> Indeed, each person's right to seek opportunities for the work necessary for the sustenance and development of himself and his family must be recognized, even beyond national and continental borders. This certainly does not exclude the legitimacy of regulation of immigration in the light of the common good of each individual nation, to be considered, however, in the context of the other nations of the world (*L'Osservatore Romano*, 1990).

Few church writings address the specifics or permissible immigration limits, or what constitutes the global common good individual nations must seek. Rome has explicitly denounced restrictions by wealthy nations that serve no other purpose than to protect their own affluence. Rome also enjoins affluent nations to commit at least two percent of GNP [gross national product] to assist developing nations, to set up structures to welcome immigrants and integrate them into society (while respecting the immigrants' loyalty to their ethnic and cultural roots), and to abstain from brain-draining and capital-draining migration policies (*Final Document*, 1991).

The American Catholic hierarchy and immigration

The American Catholic bishops have been more militant than Rome itself in questioning the legitimacy of American immigration law.

The United States' size and abundance of wealth, and its immigrant traditions, make it comparable to the thoughtless "rich man" of the biblical parable who is judged for his neglect of the needs of the beggar Lazarus (Luke 16: 19-31). The bishops' fervor stems from atavistic memories of the American church's own immigrant origins while revealing a radicalization of outlook.

The church's outlook on migration is one-of-a-piece with its ostrich-like attitude on world population growth.

Vatican Councils I and II enlarged the powers of national bishops' councils, and triggered outspoken activism within the American hierarchy on social and economic issues. Much of the subsequent outpouring of bishops' high minded statements on migration, culture, economics and foreign and defense policy has been a genuine welling up of Christian witness. Some has been pure hubris, combined with a need to compensate for the bishops' relative powerlessness on such critical church issues as contraception, abortion, ordination and empowerment of women, or reform of the priesthood.

The Catholic left's influence has also heightened the bishops' discomfort with U.S. foreign and immigration policy. The "preferential option for the poor" proclaimed in Latin American liberation theology captured the imagination of many progressive American Catholics. Its rhetoric injected notions of class struggle and class envy into the U.S. church's world view. For some this preferential option means a priority for the world's poor in immigration and the rejection of the distinctions between political and economic refugees.

For some thinkers, the exploitation of sending nations by American capitalism or the presumed support of repressive third world regimes by U.S. diplomacy has obligated the United States to accept immigrants (Christiansen, 1988). Such reasoning informed the crusade of the "sanctuary movement" to smuggle Central American illegal aliens into the U.S. in obedience to a "higher law."

U.S. bishops as a group neither endorsed nor condemned the sanctuary movement. Some individually supported it. Pope John Paul II seemed to endorse the movement in a vague statement during his 1987 visit to San Antonio, Texas (*New York Times*, 1987)—an endorsement a Vatican press spokesman claimed was never intended.

Committed to the preferential option for the poor, the hierarchy's recognition of the state's right to restrict immigration "for the common good" tends to vanish altogether. Archbishop Roger Mahony of Los Angeles, who presides over the United States' largest concentration of illegal aliens, put it in these terms:

> If the question is between the right of a nation to control its borders and the right of a person to emigrate in order to seek safe haven from hunger or violence (or both), we believe that the first right must give way to the second (Mahony, 1987).

For the bishops, enforcement of internal immigration controls, such as employer sanctions [which prohibit employers from hiring illegal immigrants], are also morally questionable. Archbishop Mahony in 1987 pledged to work with other groups "to develop new, creative employment for all our people, regardless of their standing under the new law." With his support, Los Angeles developed facilities for job placement of undocumented day laborers, a direct challenge to the intent of sanctions (*Tidings*, 1987).

In 1988 the National Conference of Catholic Bishops restated its opposition to employer sanctions because its original condition, a universal amnesty [for illegal residents], had not been met. The bishops affirmed that the right to migrate for work cannot be simply ignored in the exercise of a nation's sovereign right to control its own borders—resuscitating a doctrine they had been willing to overlook in the 1986 legislative bargaining. "The church," they noted, "must be the first to insist that love knows no borders" (*National Conference*, 1988). The bishops' staff arm, the Catholic Refugee and Migration Service, is a major participant in the coalition now lobbying for the repeal of employer sanctions.

Moral absolutes meet the secular world

While the Holy Spirit may have had a hand in creating it, such a formidable body of doctrine is not likely to be free of inconsistencies, contradictions, omissions and selective applications. Some of these inconsistencies themselves illuminate the problem of applying the selfless moral absolutes of the eternal to the disorderly, complex and competitive secular world. They point up the intractable nature of such issues as population growth, resources and stewardship, the moral efficacy of the nation-state, and the ever-intrusive question of what is God's and what is Caesar's.

To their credit, Vatican teachings on immigration at the outset recognized that "overpopulation" in fact occurs and can magnify human hardship. Too many people for the available resources indeed justified emigration. But this logic lapsed in the case of the receiving countries: immigration limits are not permissible for societies seeking to balance their populations and resources. Acknowledgement of overpopulation is rare now in church pronouncements, which in recent years have taken refuge in cornucopian economics (see Kasun, 1988). The church's outlook on migration is one-of-a-piece with its ostrich-like attitude on world population growth.

In recent years the bishops and Rome itself have said less and less about the Vatican's 1969 injunction to immigrants to absorb the language and customs of the host country to aid their integration. Instead, church leaders have joined in the rising disdain for the concept of the "melting pot" and official-English laws, and have affirmed diversity and cultural pluralism as moral ends in themselves.

The Vatican's distrust of the nation-state is centuries old, but not always consistent. While Pope John XXIII in 1958 urged supranational action to protect migrants' rights, his successor in 1992 played *realpolitik* to keep the international community from addressing the environmental costs of population growth at a 1992 U.N. Conference [on global environmental issues] at Rio de Janeiro. Nation-states do in fact act in their own best interests. The Vatican, a recognized sovereign state, did so in Rio; and it does so in governing its own tiny territory. No immigration is permitted and no refugees are accepted for resettlement.

Church leaders are wont to prescribe moral public policies, but with minimum responsibility for the costs or outcomes that temporal leaders must grapple with.

As the most "affluent" nation-state, the United States' immigration policies come under special church scrutiny. The rich United States is obliged to accept the world's poor. But the unevenness (indeed, the decline) of U.S. affluence is ignored. The nation has more than 30 million poor people, many of them recent immigrants. Perhaps these are our nation's own biblical "strangers among us" whom justice must give first claim on our resources.

Oddly, the church leadership that first championed trade unionism in the 1891 encyclical *Rerum Novarum* now preaches tolerance of a heavy illegal immigration that destroys trade unions, undercuts workers' rights, and increases income inequality. While unions were seen by Pope Leo XIII as justified in seeking to control the supply of labor, nation-states are not so justified in conducting their immigration policies. The international human rights the church promotes, such as free migration, must be weighed against other human rights of equal or greater validity—such as basic government services, domestic tranquility, job security, a decent quality of life and a sustainable environment.

The tough task of managing immigration highlights other contradictions between church teachings and church actions. Church leaders increasingly reject the international border as morally dubious. But U.S. church lobbyists arguing for the repeal of employer sanctions have spoken out for a larger border patrol (Ryscavage, 1992). Similarly, a U.S. church bureaucracy that lobbied zealously for the 1980 Refugee Act now works with equal zeal against one of that act's central principles: the priority of "political" refugees over "economic" ones. Church teachings initially conceded that immigration which deprived less developed nations of their capital or their talent was morally unjustifiable. Not much has been heard about that lately among Catholic immigration advocates. Church lobbyists in Washington have tended to push, as in the cases of El Salvador and Haiti, for mass catch-all legalization and asylum arrangements, with little concern for the differing motives and conditions of individual migrants.

Charity and responsibility

The practice here is not new in Christendom: church leaders are wont to prescribe moral public policies, but with minimum responsibility for the costs or outcomes that temporal leaders must grapple with. A legitimate mission of church, mosque and synagogue is to remind nations of the general moral principles that must underlie sound policy. This worthy role is missing when the church becomes just one more pressure group, in Washington or at the U.N., demanding specific actions. The dividing line between moral exhortation and moral blackmail is blurred.

American bishops may have to rearrange their diocesan charity budgets, but Caesar, not the clerics, will ultimately count the cost to South Florida and the federal treasury for settling and integrating 100,000 or more Haitian boat people. Nor is the hierarchy troubled by the search for revenues to overcome California's multi-billion-dollar budget deficit, aggravated by the massive immigration of the 1980s. More disturbing is the bishops' indifference to the hidden costs to America's poor of mass migrations into key cities such as Miami and Los Angeles. Rather, the Roman Catholic church as an institution has gained materially from heavy refugee flows because of contracts with the federal government to provide resettlement services. Catholic and other religious lobbyists and advocacies are commendably charitable, but too often with the goods of others.

The Bible has much to say about charity and the ancient, balancing virtues of caution, prudence, responsible stewardship and the simple fact of scarcity that compels us all to "count the cost." Worth remembering is that the Good Samaritan, when he practiced an act of compassion, unlike many of our era's altruists, was fully accountable himself for its resource consequences: "He took out two pence, gave them to the innkeeper and said unto him take care of him; and whatsoever thou spendest more, when I come again I will repay thee" (Luke 10: 35). He didn't transfer the financial burden of his compassion to others.

So it is that the church is "in the world and not of it." But human beings in their search for peace, order and justice build institutions such as governments that inevitably must be both in the world and of it.

References

Bikales, G., "A New Immigration Ethic for the U.S.: Updating the Golden Rule for the Global Village," *The Humanist*, March/April 1983.

Buckley, W.F., Opinion piece in the *New York Times*, September 29, 1987.

Christiansen, D., "Sacrament of Unity: Ethical Issues in Pastoral Care of Migrants and Refugees," in *Today's Immigrants and Refugees: A Christian Understanding*. Washington: U.S. Catholic Conference, 1988.

Cultural Pluralism in the United States: A Statement Issued by the U.S. Catholic Conference, April 14, 1980. Washington: U.S. Catholic Conference.

Kasun, J., *The War Against Population: The Economics and Ideology of Popula-*

tion Control. San Francisco: Ignatius Press, 1988.

Mahony, R., "Catholic Social Teaching on Immigration," *The Tidings*, April 1987.

Mahony, R., *A New Partnership: A Pastoral Statement Highlighting National Migration Week*. Archdiocese of Los Angeles, January 4, 1987.

Miller, P.D., "Israel as Host to Strangers" in *Today's Immigrants and Refugees: A Christian Understanding*. Washington: U.S. Catholic Conference, 1988.

National Conference of Catholic Bishops: Policy Statement on Employer Sanctions, November 1988. Washington: U.S. Catholic Conference, 1988.

Niebuhr, Reinhold, *Moral Man and Immoral Society*. New York: Scribner's, 1960.

Pope John Paul II, *The Ecological Crisis, A Common Responsibility*. Washington: U.S. Catholic Conference, 1990.

"Pope Lauds Those Who Aid Refugees of Latin America," *New York Times*, August 14, 1987.

Pope Paul VI, *On the Development of Peoples (Populorum Progressio)*. Washington: U.S. Catholic Conference, 1967.

Ryscavage, R., *Testimony on Behalf of the U.S. Catholic Conference on S.1734, Legislation to Repeal Employer Sanctions* before the U.S. Senate Committee on the Judiciary, April 3,1992.

Sacred Congregation of Bishops: Instructions on the Pastoral Care of People Who Migrate, Vatican City, August 22, 1969. Washington: U.S. Catholic Conference, 1969.

"Solidarity with the New Migrations," Excerpts from the *Final Document of the Third International Congress of Pastoral Care of Migrants and Refugees, Vatican City, 1991*, in *Migration World*, Vol. XX, No. 2.

Tomasi, S.M., "Immigrants Today: A Call to Solidarity," *Migration World*, Vol. XIX, No. 5.

"Universal Declaration of Human Rights," New York: United Nations, Office of Public Information, December 10, 1948.

"We Must Stand with Our People," *The Tidings*, April 24, 1987.

Zall, B., "The U.S. Refugee Industry: Doing Well by Doing Good," in Simcox, D.E. (ed.), *U.S. Immigration in the 1980s: Reappraisal and Reform*. Boulder, CO: Westview, 1988.

10

Immigration to the United States Should Be Increased

Julian L. Simon

Julian L. Simon, a teacher of business administration at the University of Maryland, College Park, is renowned for his conviction that large-scale immigration is beneficial in a free-market economy. He details the positive effects of immigration in his well-known book The Economic Consequences of Immigration.

Increased immigration to the United States would contribute to the country's technological advancement, help provide for the nation's labor needs, increase tax revenues, and improve U.S. competitiveness in the world economy. Contrary to common misconceptions, immigrants do not harm the U.S. economy by abusing welfare and displacing native workers. Immigrants pay more in taxes than they receive in social service benefits, and they improve the job market by increasing the demand for labor. In order to boost the nation's productivity and sharpen its technological edge, the United States should change its immigration policies to favor skilled workers. Moreover, each year the country should increase its number of legal immigrants by 500,000.

By increasing somewhat the flow of immigrants—from about 600,000 to about 750,000 admissions per year—the immigration legislation [Immigration Act] passed by Congress late in 1990 will improve the standard of living of native-born Americans. The bill represents a sea change in public attitude toward immigration; it demonstrates that substantially increasing immigration is politically possible now. That's all good news, and we should celebrate it.

The bad news is that the legislation does not *greatly* increase immigration. The new rate is still quite low by historical standards. A much larger increase in numbers—even to, say, only half the rate relative to population size that the United States accepted around the turn of the century—would surely increase our standard of living even more.

The political problem for advocates of immigration is to avoid the let-

Julian L. Simon, "The Case for Greatly Increased Immigration." Reprinted with permission of the author and *The Public Interest*, No. 102 (Winter 1991), pp. 89-103, ©1991 by National Affairs, Inc.

down to be expected after the passage of this first major legal-immigration bill in a quarter-century. And since the new law seems to contemplate additional legislation (by providing for a commission to collect information on immigration), it is important to educate the public about how immigration benefits the nation as well as the immigrants.

Increased immigration presents the United States with an opportunity to realize many national goals with a single stroke. It is a safe and sure path—open to no other nation—to achieve all of these benefits: 1) a sharply increased rate of technological advance, spurred by the addition of top scientific talent from all over the world; 2) satisfaction of business's demand for the labor that the baby-bust generation makes scarce; 3) reduction of the burden that retirees impose upon the ever-shrinking cohort of citizens of labor-force age, who must support the Social Security System; 4) rising tax revenues—resulting from the increase in the proportion of workers to retirees—that will provide the only painless way of shrinking and perhaps even eliminating the federal deficit; 5) improvement in our competitive position vis-á-vis Japan, Europe, and the rest of the world; 6) a boost to our image abroad, stemming from immigrants' connections with their relatives back home, and from the remittances that they send back to them; and 7) not least, the opportunity given to additional people to enjoy the blessings of life in the United States.

All the U.S. need do to achieve these benefits is further to relax its barriers against skilled immigrants. Talented and energetic people want to come here. Yet we do not greatly avail ourselves of this golden opportunity, barring the door to many of the most economically productive workers in the world.

If immigration is such an across-the-board winner, why aren't we welcoming skilled and hardworking foreigners with open arms? These are some of the reasons: 1) The public is ignorant of the facts to be presented here; it therefore charges immigrants with increasing unemployment, abusing welfare programs, and lowering the quality of our work force. 2) Various groups fear that immigrants would harm their particular interests; the groups are less concerned with the welfare of the country as a whole. 3) Well-organized lobbies oppose immigration, which receives little organized support. 4) Nativism, which may or may not be the same as racism in any particular case, continues to exert an appeal.

The dimensions of present-day immigration

The most important issue is the total number of immigrants allowed into the United States. It is important to keep our eyes fixed on this issue, because it tends to get obscured in emotional discussions of the desirability of reuniting families, the plight of refugees, the geographic origin and racial composition of our immigrant population, the needs of particular industries, the illegality of some immigration, and so on.

The Federation for American Immigration Reform (FAIR)—whose rhetoric I shall use as illustration—says that "[i]mmigration to the United States is at record levels." This claim is simply false: Figure I shows the absolute numbers of legal immigrants over the decades. The recent inflow clearly is far below the inflow around the turn of the century—even though it includes the huge number of immigrants who took advantage of the 1986 amnesty [offered by the Immigration Reform and Control Act to illegal immigrants who had lived in the United States since before 1982];

they are classified as having entered in 1989, although most of them actually arrived before 1980. Even the inclusion of illegal immigrants does not alter the fact that there is less immigration now than in the past.

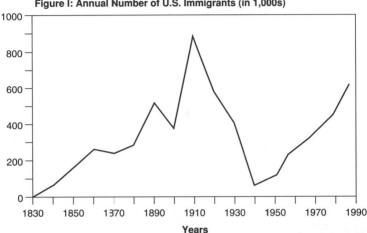

Figure I: Annual Number of U.S. Immigrants (in 1,000s)

Economically speaking, more relevant than these absolute numbers is the volume of immigration as a proportion of the native population, as shown in Figure II. Between 1901 and 1910 immigrants arrived at the yearly rate of 10.4 per thousand U.S. population, whereas between 1981 and 1987 the rate was only 2.5 per thousand of the population. So the recent flow is less than a fourth as heavy as it was in that earlier period. Australia and Canada admit three times that many immigrants as a proportion of their populations.

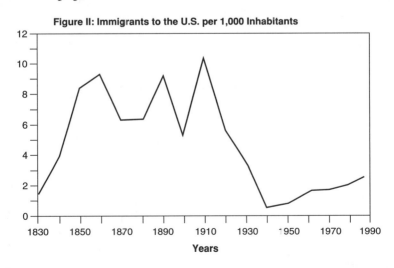

Figure II: Immigrants to the U.S. per 1,000 Inhabitants

Another way to think about the matter: in 1910, 14.6 percent of the population was born abroad, but in 1980 less than 6 percent of us were. Not only is the present stock of immigrants much smaller proportionally than it was earlier, but it also is a small proportion considered by itself. We tend to think of ourselves as a "nation of immigrants," but less than one out of fifteen people now in the U.S. was born abroad, including those who arrived many years ago. Who would guess that the U.S. has a smaller share of foreign-born residents than many countries that we tend to think have closed homogeneous populations—including Great Britain, Switzerland, France, and Germany? We are a nation not of immigrants, but rather of the descendants of immigrants.

Furthermore, the absorption of immigrants is much easier now than it was in earlier times. One has only to read the history of the Pilgrims in Plymouth Colony to realize the enormity of the immediate burden that each new load of immigrants represented. But it is the essence of an advanced society that it can more easily handle material problems than can technically primitive societies. With every year it becomes easier for us to make the material adjustments that an increase in population requires. That is, immigrant assimilation becomes ever less of an economic problem—all the more reason that the proportion of immigrants now seems relatively small, compared with what it was in the past.

Unfortunately, despite recent changes favoring skilled immigrants, our present admissions policy remains largely nepotistic. Most visas are granted to foreigners who have family connections here. Even with the 1990 legislation, the U.S. will admit only about 110,000 people—perhaps 20 percent of all immigrants—on the basis of their job skills. Compare our policy with Australia's, which admits almost 50 percent of its immigrants according to "economic" criteria, and only 30 percent as relatives of citizens. Many of those whom we admit via family preferences also are skilled, of course, but it would be beneficial to us as well as fair to deserving foreigners to admit more people on the basis of merit alone. Indeed, George Borjas of the University of California at Santa Barbara has presented evidence that the economic "quality" of immigrants with given levels of education has declined in recent decades—though the magnitude of the decline remains controversial; the likeliest explanation for the decline is an increase in the proportion of immigrants who are admitted as relatives rather than on their merits alone. On the other hand, Harriet Duleep of the U.S. Civil Rights Commission has recently shown that despite the different admissions policies of the U.S. and Canada (which uses a point system), immigration affects the economies of the two countries similarly—probably because families carefully evaluate the economic potential of relatives before deciding to bring them in.

For years, phony inflated estimates of the stocks and flows of illegal immigrants were bandied about by opponents of immigration in order to muddy the waters. Since the 1986 Simpson-Mazzoli law's amnesty we know that the numbers are actually quite modest, much lower than even the "mainstream" estimates cited in the press. So that scare no longer serves as an effective red herring for opponents of immigration.

The costs and benefits of immigration

Now let us consider the costs and benefits of immigration—even though economic issues may not be the real heart of the matter, often serving only as a smoke screen to conceal the true motives for opposition. Only thus can one explain why the benefits of immigration do not produce more open policies. Because opponents of immigration wield economic arguments to justify their positions, however, we must consider their assertions.

[Malthusianism is the theory that population increases faster than food supplies; and unless it is controlled by man or natural disaster, poverty is inevitable.] Malthusian objections to immigration begin with "capital dilution." The supposed "law of diminishing returns"—which every economics text explains should not be thought of as a law—causes output per worker to fall. The "law" is so marvelously simple, direct, and commonsensical that it easily seduces thought—especially among academics, for whom such abstractions are bread and butter. Its simplicity also makes the Malthusian notion excellent fare for the family newspaper. In contrast, the arguments that demonstrate the inapplicability of Malthusian capital dilution in the context of immigration are relatively complex and indirect. As a consequence, simple—though incorrect—Malthusianism easily attracts adherents.

We are a nation not of immigrants, but rather of the descendants of immigrants.

Nowadays, however, the most important capital is human capital—education and skills, which people own themselves and carry with them—rather than capitalist-supplied physical capital. The bugaboo of production capital has been laid to rest by the experience of the years since World War II, which taught economists that, aside from the shortest-run considerations, physical capital does not pose a major constraint to economic growth. It is human capital that is far more important in a country's development. And immigrants supply their own human capital.

The main real cost that immigration imposes on natives is the extra capital needed for additional schools and hospitals. But this cost turns out to be small relative to benefits, in considerable part because we finance such construction with bond issues, so that we operate largely on a pay-as-you-go basis. Immigrants therefore pay much of their share.

The supposed cost that most captures the public's imagination, of course, is welfare payments. According to popular belief, no sooner do immigrants arrive than they become public charges, draining welfare money from the American taxpayers, and paying no taxes.

Solid evidence gives the lie to this charge. In an analysis of Census Bureau data I found that, aside from Social Security and Medicare, about as much money is spent on welfare services and schooling for immigrant families as for citizens. When programs for the elderly are included, immigrant families receive far *less* in public services than natives. During the first five years in the U.S., the average immigrant family receives $1,400 in welfare and schooling (in 1975 dollars), compared with the $2,300 received by the average native family. The receipts gradually become equal over several decades. Athur Akhbari of St. Mary's College in Canada has shown that recent Canadian data produce almost identical results. And Duleep's finding that the economic results of Canadian and U.S. immigration are quite similar, despite the different admissions systems, adds weight to the conclusion that U.S. immigrants pay much more in taxes than they receive in benefits.

Of course there must be some systematic abuses of the welfare system by immigrants. But our legislative system is capable of devising adequate

remedies. Even now there are provisions in the Immigration and Naturalization Act that deny visas to aliens who are "likely to become public
charges" and provide for the deportation of immigrants who have within
five years after entry become public charges "from causes not affirma-
tively shown to have arisen after entry."

As to illegal immigrants and welfare, FAIR typically says that "[t]ax-
payers are hurt by having to pay more for social services." Ironically, several surveys—for example, one by Sidney Weintraub and Gilberto Carde-
nas of the University of Texas—show that illegals are even heavier net
contributors to the public coffers than legal immigrants; many illegals are
in the U.S. only temporarily and are therefore without families, and they
are often afraid to apply for services for fear of being apprehended. Illegals do, however, pay taxes.

Some cities and states with disproportionately high immigration do
incur significant costs and complications when immigrants first arrive.
They deserve sympathy and perhaps federal assistance, though officials
should note that immigrants' federal taxes will later effectively pay for
such temporary assistance.

The non-threat of displaced native workers

The most dramatic argument against immigration—the bogeyman in the
mind of organized labor, which has been its most powerful political op-
ponent since the nineteenth century—has been that foreigners take jobs
held by natives and thereby increase native unemployment. The logic is
simple: if the number of jobs is fixed, and immigrants occupy some jobs,
there must be fewer available jobs for natives.

In the shortest run, the demand for any particular sort of worker is indeed inflexible. Therefore, additional immigrants in a given occupation
must to some degree lower wages and/or increase unemployment in that
occupation. For example, the large recent influx of foreign physicians increases the competition that U.S. physicians face, lowering their earnings.
But because immigrants come with a variety of skills, workers in most occupations feel little impact. And in the longer run, workers in most occupations are not injured at all.

A good-sized body of competent recent research shows that immigration does not exacerbate unemployment, even among directly competing
groups; in California, for instance, immigrants have not increased unemployment among blacks and women. And the research, done by several
independent scholars from a variety of angles, uses several kinds of data.
For example, Stephen Moore and I systematically studied immigration's
effects upon overall unemployment, by looking at the changes in unemployment in various U.S. cities that have experienced different levels of
unemployment. We found that if there is displacement, it is too little to
be observable.

The explanation is that immigrants not only take jobs, but also create them. Their purchases increase the demand for labor, leading to new
hires roughly equal in number to the immigrant workers. Immigrants also
create jobs directly by opening new businesses. A Canadian government
survey of immigrants, which should also describe U.S. experience, found
that almost 5 percent—91 of the 1746 males and 291 single females in its
panel sample—had started businesses within their first three years in
Canada. Not only did they employ themselves, but they also employed

others, creating a total of 606 jobs. Thus the total of 2037 immigrants personally created roughly 30 percent as many jobs as they collectively held. Furthermore, these numbers surely rose rapidly after the three-year study period; after one year 71 self-employed immigrants had created 264 jobs, compared with the 91 immigrant entrepreneurs and 606 jobs observed after three years.

U.S. immigrants pay much more in taxes than they receive in benefits.

We can interpret this result as follows: even if one native Canadian was pushed out of a preexisting job by every five immigrants—an improbably high number—this effect would be more than made up for by the new jobs, occupied by natives, created by the immigrants' businesses.

The businesses that immigrants start are at first small, of course. But surprisingly, small businesses are the most important source of new jobs. And immigrant entrepreneurs tend to succeed in a dynamic economy, because they are innovative and mobile.

Furthermore, potential immigrants are well aware of labor-market conditions in the U.S., and they tend not to come if there is little demand for their skills. Natives tend not to be harmed even in the few industries—like the restaurant and hotel businesses—in which immigrants concentrate, because natives do not want jobs in these industries. Evidence for this comes from experiments conducted by the Immigration and Naturalization Service and San Diego County. In one case, 2154 illegal aliens were removed from jobs, but the California State Human Resources Agency had almost no success in filling the jobs with U.S. citizens.

Wages are admittedly pushed downward somewhat in industries and localities in which immigrants are concentrated. Barton Smith and Robert Newman of the University of Houston found that adjusted wages are 8 percent lower in the Texas border cities in which the proportion of Mexicans is relatively high. Much of the apparent difference is accounted for by a lower cost of living in the border cities, however. And because immigrants tend to be heterogeneous in their skills, their presence does not disproportionately affect any particular industry; and of course salaries rise in the occupations that few immigrants enter. (Indeed, if immigrants were spread evenly throughout all occupations, wages would not fall in any occupation.) At the same time, immigrants, who consume a wide variety of goods and services, increase the demand for labor across the range of occupations.

Tax payments

If immigrants paid relatively little in taxes they might still burden natives, despite using fewer welfare services. But data on family earnings, which allow us to estimate tax payments, show that this is not at all the case.

Immigrants pay more than their share of taxes. Within three to five years, immigrant-family earnings reach and pass those of the average American family. The tax and welfare data together indicate that, on balance, an immigrant family enriches natives by contributing an average of $1,300 or more per year (in 1975 dollars) to the public coffers during its stay in the U.S. Evaluating the future stream of these contributions as one would a dam or harbor, the present value of an immigrant family—discounted at the risk-free interest rate of 3 percent—adds up to almost two years' earnings for a native family head. This means that the economic activities of an average immigrant family reduce the taxes of a native head of household enough to advance his or her possible date of retirement by two years.

Immigrants not only take jobs, but also create them.

Curiously, contemporary welfare-state policies render immigration more beneficial to natives than it was in earlier times when welfare was mainly voluntary. There are two main reason why today's immigrants make net contributions to the public coffers. First, far from being tired, huddled masses, immigrants tend to come when they are young, strong, and vibrant, at the start of their work lives. For example, perhaps 46 percent of immigrants are in the prime labor-force ages of twenty to thirty-nine, compared with perhaps 26 percent of natives. And only 4 percent of immigrants are aged sixty or over, compared with about 15 percent of natives. Second, many immigrants are well educated and have well-paying skills that produce hefty tax contributions.

Because immigrants arrive in the early prime of their work lives, they ward off a major looming threat to U.S. economic well-being. This threat is the graying of the population, which means that each working native has an increasing burden of retired dependents to support. In 1900, there were five and one-half people aged twenty-five to fifty-four for each person aged sixty and above, whereas the Census Bureau projects that in the year 2000 the ratio will shrink to two and one-half to one—resulting in a burden that will be more than twice as heavy on workers.

Being predominantly youthful adults, immigrants mitigate this looming problem of more retired natives being supported by fewer workers. Indeed, immigration is the only practical way to alleviate the burden of increasing dependency that native workers would otherwise feel.

In the public sphere this means that immigrants immediately lessen the Social Security burden upon native workers. (The same holds for the defense burden, of course.) And if there is a single factor currently complicating the government's economic policies, it is the size of Social Security payments and other assistance to the aged. Immigration—and the resulting increase in tax payments by immigrants—provides the only way to reduce the federal budget deficit without making painful cuts in valued services.

Boosting productivity

Most important in the long run is the boost that immigrants give to productivity. Though hard to pin down statistically, the beneficial impact of immigration upon productivity is likely to dwarf all other effects after these additional workers and consumers have been in the country a few years. Some of the productivity increase comes from immigrants working in industries and laboratories that are at the forefront of world technology. We benefit along with others from the contribution to world productivity in, say, genetic engineering that immigrants could not make in their home countries. More immigrants mean more workers, who will think up productivity-enhancing ideas. As Soichiro Honda (of motorcycle and auto fame) said: "Where 100 people think, there are 100 powers; if 1,000 people think, there are 1,000 powers."

It is well to remember that the development of the atomic bomb hinged on the participation of such immigrants as Enrico Fermi, John von Neumann, and Stan Ulam, among many others. Contemporary newspaper stories continue this historical saga, noting the disproportionate numbers of Vietnamese and other Asian immigrant youths who achieve distinction in competitions such as the Westinghouse Science Talent Search. Ben Wattenberg and Karl Zinsmeister of the American Enterprise Institute write that among the forty 1988 finalists, "22 were foreign-born or children of foreign-born parents: from Taiwan, China, Korea, India, Guyana, Poland, Trinidad, Canada, Peru, Iran, Vietnam and Honduras." They also note that one-fourth of recent valedictorians and salutatorians in San Diego have been Vietnamese, and that thirteen of the seventeen public high school valedictorians in Boston in 1989 were foreign born. Sometimes it seems as if such names as Wang Computers and Steve Chen dominate our most vigorous industry.

The bottom line

An economist always owes the reader a cost-benefit assessment for policy analysis. So I combined the most important elements pertaining to legal immigrants with a simple macroeconomic model, making reasonable assumptions where necessary. The net effect is slightly negative for the early years, but four or five years later the net effect turns positive and large. And when we tote up future costs and benefits, the rate of "investment" return from immigrants to the citizen public is about 20 percent per annum—a good return for any portfolio.

Does all this seem to be a far-out minority view? In 1990 the American Immigration Institute [an immigration advocacy organization] surveyed prominent economists—all the ex-presidents of the American Economic Association [an organization of individuals interested in economics], and then-members of the Council of Economic Advisers—about immigration. Economists ought to understand the economic effects of immigration better than others, so their views are of special interest. More than four-fifths of the respondents said that immigration has a very favorable impact on economic growth; none said that its impact is unfavorable. Almost three-fourths said that illegals have a positive economic impact. And almost all agree that recent immigrants have had the same kind of impact as immigrants in the past.

The real reasons for opposition

I began by citing various reasons for our failure to take in more immigrants, despite the clear-cut benefits of doing so. The first is ignorance of the benefits described above. Second is the opposition by special interests, such as organized labor (which wants to restrict competition for jobs) and ethnic groups (whose members often fear that immigration will cause their proportion of the population to decrease). The third reason is well-organized opposition to immigration and a total lack of organized support for it.

FAIR, for example, has a large budget—it amassed $2,000,000 in revenues in 1989—and a large staff. It supports letter-writing campaigns to newspapers and legislators, gets its representatives onto television and radio, and is in the rolodex of every journalist who writes on the subject. Several other organizations play a similar role. On the other side, until recently no organization advocated more immigration generally. Now at least there is the fledgling American Immigration Institute; and the de Tocqueville Institute did excellent work on immigration in 1989 and 1990, before taking on other issues. [The American Immigration Institute has ceased operation since this article was written.]

The fourth check to immigration is nativism or racism, a motive that often lies beneath the surface of the opposition's arguments.

Rita Simon of American University, who has studied the history of public opinion toward immigrants, has found that the arguments against immigration have remained eerily identical. In the first half of the nineteenth century, Irish immigrants in New York and Boston were seen as the unassimilable possessors of all bad qualities. One newspaper wrote: "America has become the sewer into which the pollutions of European jails are emptied." Another asked: "Have we not a right to protect ourselves against the ravenous dregs of anarchy and crime, the tainted swarms of pauperism and vice Europe shakes on our shores from her diseased robes?"

The 1884 platform of the Democratic party stated its opposition to the "importation of foreign labor or the admission of servile races unfitted by habit, training, religion or kindred for absorption into the great body of our people or for the citizenship which our laws confer."

Francis Walker, Commissioner General of the Immigration Service, wrote in 1896:

> The question today is . . . protecting the American rate of wages, the American standard of living, and the quality of American citizenship from degradation through the tumultuous access of vast throngs of ignorant and brutalized peasantry from the countries of Eastern and Southern Europe.

In the 1920s the *Saturday Evening Post* also directed fear and hatred at the "new immigrants" from Southern and Eastern Europe: "More than a third of them cannot read and write; generally speaking they have been very difficult to assimilate. . . . They have been hot beds of dissent, unrest, sedition and anarchy."

Although statements like these are no longer acceptable in public, many people still privately sympathize with such views. One can see the traces in nativist codewords that accuse immigrants of "disturbing national homogeneity" and "changing our national culture."

Improving our policies

In addition to admitting more immigrants into the United States, we should also consider instituting other desirable changes in policy. Specifically, we must go further to increase the benefits that accrue to the United States from the inflow of highly educated people with high productive potential—especially people with technical skills. To its credit, the 1990 legislation will increase the flow of talented people by increasing the proportion of immigrants who are admitted because of their economic characteristics rather than their familial ties to U.S. citizens. This was worth doing to reduce nepotistic "family connections" admissions, and to treat meritorious applicants without such connections more fairly.

The new system does not greatly increase the flow of highly skilled people, however. An additional 100,000 or so immigrants will be admitted under the new provisions for economic selection; only 40,000 will be skilled people, the other 60,000 being their dependents. The overall increase in numbers admitted will yield perhaps another 30,000 highly skilled people. This is still only a small—though a most valuable—increment to our economy.

The 1990 legislation also contains a beneficial provision allowing entry to people who will invest a million dollars and create employment for ten Americans. Although this provision will not be as profitable for natives as an outright sale of the opportunity to immigrate, as permitted by some other countries, it does move in the right direction. But the new law does not go far enough; it permits entry to a maximum of only 10,000 persons per year under this provision—a piddling number by any standard.

> *The best way for the U.S. to boost its rate of technological advance, and to raise its standard of living, is simply to take in more immigrants.*

Another policy that the U.S. might employ is simply to give permanent-resident visas to foreigners studying in the U.S. Many foreign students already find ways to remain under the present rules—about half of them students of engineering and science. And even more foreign graduates would remain if they could, which would push up our rate of progress even more.

Furthermore, if young foreigners knew that they could remain in the United States after completing their education here, more would choose to study here. This would provide multiple benefits to the United States. Given assurance that they could remain, these students could pay more realistic tuition rates than are now charged, which would benefit U.S. universities. And these increased rates would enable universities to expand their programs to serve both foreign and native students better. Best of all would be the increased number of highly competent scientific and managerial workers who would be part of the American work force.

In addition, a larger number of students requires a larger number of professors. And a larger number of openings for professors, especially in such fields as engineering and science, would attract more of the world's best scientists from abroad. This would enhance the process that has brought so many foreigners who subsequently won Nobel prizes to the U.S.—to the advantage as well as the honor of this country.

Political advantages

Political power and economic well-being are intimately related; a nation's international standing is heavily influenced by its economic situation. And today the future of any country—especially of a major country that is in the vanguard with respect to production and living standards—depends entirely on its progress in knowledge, skill, and productivity. This is more true now than in the past, because technology changes more rapidly than in earlier times. Even a single invention can speedily alter a country's economic or military future—consider, for example, the atom bomb or the computer—as no invention could in the past, even the invention of the gun. That's why immigration safely, cheaply, and surely provides the U.S. with perhaps the greatest opportunity that a country has ever had to surpass its political rivals.

And the best way for the U.S. to boost its rate of technological advance, and to raise its standard of living, is simply to take in more immigrants. To that end, I would suggest that the number of visas be increased by half a million per year for three years. If no major problems arise with that total (and there is no reason to expect a problem, since even another one or two million immigrants a year would still give us an admissions rate lower than we successfully coped with in earlier times, when assimilation was more difficult), then we should boost the number by another half-million, and so on, until unexpected problems arise.

Immigration policy presents the U.S. with an opportunity like the one that faced the Brooklyn Dodgers in 1947, before blacks played baseball on any major-league team. Signing Jackie Robinson and then Roy Campanella, at the price of antagonizing some players and club owners, put the Dodgers way ahead of the pack. In the case of immigration, unlike baseball, no other "team" can duplicate our feat, because immigrants mainly want to come here. All we need is the vision, guts, and ambition of Dodger general manager Branch Rickey. (A bit of his religious zeal mixed in would do no harm.)

Can we see our national interest clearly enough to reject unfounded beliefs that some groups will lose jobs to immigrants, and to surmount the racism that remains in our society? Or will we pay a heavy price in slower growth and lessened efficiency for maintaining our prejudices and pandering to the supposed interests of groups—organized labor, environmentalists, and others—whose misguided wishes will not benefit even them in the long run?

11

Immigration Policy Should Reflect Economic Globalization

Saskia Sassen

Saskia Sassen is a professor of urban planning at Columbia University in New York City and the author of The Global City: New York, London, & Tokyo *(Princeton Univ. Press, 1991) and* Cities in a World Economy *(Pine Forge: Sage, 1994).*

While the United States and other developed countries are opening their economies to foreign investment and trade, their immigration policies remain rooted in the increasingly irrelevant notions of nation-states and national borders. Immigration policies should recognize the effects on immigration patterns of global economic integration, as exemplified by regional trading blocs and systems for the internationalization of manufacturing production.

Current immigration policy in developed countries is increasingly at odds with other major policy frameworks in the international system and with the growth of global economic integration. All highly developed countries have received rapidly growing numbers of legal and undocumented immigrants over the last decade; none has found its immigration policy effective. These countries are opening up their economies to foreign investment and trade while deregulating their financial markets. In developed countries, the emergence of a new economic regime sharply reduces the role of national governments and borders in controlling international transactions. Yet the framework of immigration policy in these countries remains centered on older conceptions of the nation-state and of national borders.

How can immigration policy account for the facts of rapid economic internationalization and the corresponding transformation of national governments? This is the subject I briefly discuss here.

The 1980s saw a major shift in the global economy. In that decade, the developed countries opened their economies to foreign investment, international financial markets, and imports of goods and services; deregulation

Saskia Sassen, "Immigrants in a Global Economy," *Crossroads*, November 1993. Reprinted with permission.

and internationalization of a growing range of economic activities became hallmarks of economic policy. As economic doors have opened to others, many developing countries have implemented export-oriented growth strategies. Export-manufacturing zones and the sale of once–public-sector firms on world markets became key venues for this internationalization.

Global economic trends engendered a new framework for national economic policy-making. This new framework is evident in the formation of regional trading blocs: the U.S.-Canada Free Trade Agreement, the European Community (EC), the new trading blocs being formed in Southeast Asia as well as the NAFTA [North American Free Trade Agreement]. At the heart of this framework is a new conception of the role of national borders. Borders no longer are sites for imposing levies. Rather, they are transmitting membranes guaranteeing the free flow of goods, capital and information. Eighteenth-century concepts of free trade assumed freedom of movement between distinct national economies; 21st-century concepts of free trade are about an economy which is itself global, and about governments that coordinate rather than control economic activities.

Borders no longer are sites for imposing levies. Rather, they are transmitting membranes guaranteeing the free flow of goods, capital and information.

To be sure, neither the old border-wall nor the nation-state has disappeared. The difficulties and complexities involved in this transformation are evident in the many obstacles to the ratification of the Uruguay Round of the GATT [General Agreement on Tariffs and Trade] talks, which aims at further opening economies to the circulation of services. But the relentless effort to overcome these difficulties also signals the pressure to depart from an old conception of national economic policy and the emergence of a new conception of how economic activity is to be maximized and governed.

The framework for immigration policy in the highly developed countries, on the other hand, is still rooted in the past. Immigration policy has yet to address global economic integration in the 21st century and its implications. Border-control remains the basic mechanism for regulating immigration—an increasingly troubled effort given new policies aimed at opening up national economies, such as the lifting of restrictions on foreign investment, the deregulation of financial markets, and the formation of financial free zones in major cities. Those policies amount to a partial denationalizing of national territory for the flow of capital, and they in turn globalize certain sectors of the workforce, notably the high-level transnational professional and managerial class.

Moreover, the policy framework for immigration treats the flow of labor as the result of individual actions, particularly the decision to migrate in search of better opportunities. Such a policy puts responsibility for immigration on the shoulders of immigrants. Policy commentary which speaks of an immigrant "influx" or "invasion" treats the receiving country as a passive agent. The causes for immigration appear to be outside the control or domain of receiving countries; immigration policy becomes a decision to be more or less benevolent in admitting immigrants. Absent from this understanding is the notion that the international activities of the governments or firms of receiving countries may have contributed to the formation of economic linkages with emigration countries, linkages that may function as bridges not only for capital but also for migration flows. That older view emphasizes individual "push" factors and neglects systemic linkages.

The worldwide evidence shows rather clearly that there is considerable patterning in the geography of migrations, and that the major receiving countries tend to get immigrants from their zones of influence. This holds for countries as diverse as the U.S., France or Japan. A transnational analysis of immigration contributes to its redefinition and allows us to see migrations as happening within global systems. The periods known as Pax Britannica and Pax Americana are but two representations of such transnational systems. The formation of systems for the internationalization of manufacturing production and the formation of regional trading blocs are other instances. These systems can be characterized in a multiplicity of ways: economic (the Atlantic economy of the 1800s, the EC, NAFTA); politico-military (the colonial systems of several European countries, U.S. involvement in Central America); transnational war zones (formation of massive refugee flows as a result of major European wars); cultural-ideological zones (impact in socialist countries of the image of Western democracies as offering the "good life").

Recent developments in Japan capture the intersection of economic internationalization and immigration. They also illuminate the intersection of immigration policy and reality. Japan's closed door policy has not prevented a growing influx of immigrants. Nor has its 1990 immigration law, which opens up the country to high-level foreign workers but closes it to all low-wage workers, kept out the latter. Furthermore, despite a strong anti-immigration culture, immigrants have become incorporated into various labor markets and have begun to form immigrant communities in major cities in Japan. A detailed exploration of the dynamic at work provides useful insights into immigration processes.

What makes the disparity between the framework for immigration policy and the facts of the world economy particularly urgent is that all highly developed countries have experienced sharp increases in migration of both legal and undocumented immigrants. In some countries there is a resurgence of immigration after inflows had fallen sharply in the 1970s: this is the case for Germany and Austria. In other countries, notably the U.S., immigration policy opened up the country in 1965, yet in the 1980s, the number of entries doubled compared with the 1965–1980 period. Still other countries are becoming immigration countries for the first time in their contemporary histories: this is the case with Italy and Spain, long-time emigration countries, and with Japan, a nation of deep anti-immigration beliefs and policies.

Discard old notions

A detailed analysis of cross-country immigration patterns suggests that some key notions about immigration may be inadequate, particularly the notion that the developed countries may be facing a massive invasion of people from less developed countries. These cross-country regularities suggest that there is more room for effective and equitable policies than the imagery of "invasion" allows:

1. *Emigration is a minority event in demographic terms*. Except for terror-

driven refugees, we now know that most people are reluctant to leave their home villages or towns. For example, most people in Mexico have not gone to the U.S. A minority is determined to come no matter what, while a gray area of potential emigrants may or may not leave, depending on pull factors; but the vast mass of people in a poor country are not likely to emigrate.

2. *There is considerable return migration* except when the military/ political situation in countries of origin makes it unsafe. For example, we now know that about 60 percent of Italians who left for the U.S. around the turn of the century returned to Italy.

3. Rather than an uncontrolled "invasion," what we see over time is a *tendency towards the formation of permanent settlements* for a variable share of immigrants, but never all. This tendency is likely even when there are high return rates and even when a country's policies seek to prevent permanent settlement. We see this happening in all countries receiving immigrants, including such extremely closed countries as Japan and Saudi Arabia, as well as in the more liberal Western nations.

4. No matter what the political culture and the particular migration policies of a country, *"illegal" immigration has emerged as a generalized fact in all Western economies in the post World War II era*, including Japan. This has raised a whole set of questions about the need to rethink regulatory enforcement and the sites for such enforcement.

5. *Immigration is a highly differentiated process:* it includes people seeking permanent settlement and those seeking temporary employment who want to circulate back and forth. One important question is whether recognizing these differences might facilitate the formulation of policy today. There is a growing presence of immigrants who are not searching for a new home in a new country; they think of themselves as moving in a cross-country and even global labor market. We know that when illegal immigrants are regularized, they often establish permanent residence in their country of origin and work a few months in the immigration country, an option that becomes available when they can circulate freely.

How should the new reality shape our thinking about immigration? A more comprehensive approach can provide more analytic and empirical footholds towards a better understanding of migration and towards more effective policy. The various transnational economic, cultural, political systems now evident in the world all tend to have very specific geographies. They are not planet-wide events, but occur in the relation of cities to cities, or in production chains linking factories in rather remote areas of developing countries to manufacturing and distribution centers in developed countries. Considerable migration flows within these new geographies for economic transactions. By understanding the nature of these geographies we can understand where to intervene for regulatory purposes. Further, international migrations themselves are patterned in geographic, economic and temporal terms. These two types of patterning provide maps within which to search for new policies to regulate immigration.

If immigration is partly an outcome of the actions of the governments and major private economic actors in receiving countries, the latter could conceivably recognize the migration impact of such actions and make decisions accordingly. For instance, economic policies that facilitate overseas operations of firms, particularly in developing countries, should recognize the migration impact of such operations. Economic internationalization suggests that the responsibility for immigration may not be exclusively the immigrant's. Refugee policy in some countries does lift the burden of immigration from the immigrant's shoulders. U.S. refugee policy, particularly for Indochinese refugees, does acknowledge partial responsibility on the part of the government. Clearly, in the case of economic migrations, such responsibility is far more difficult to establish, and by its nature far more indirect. As governments increasingly coordinate rather than contain economic activity, their role in immigration policy, as in other aspects of political economy, becomes elusive. Despite this complexity, the responsibilities for the consequences of globalization do not disappear. If economic internationalization contributes to migration flows, recognition of this fact can only help in designing more effective immigration policy.

12

U.S. Immigration Policy Should Not Discriminate

Peter D. Salins

Peter D. Salins is a senior fellow of the Manhattan Institute for Policy Research, a nonpartisan policy research organization, and director of the graduate program in urban affairs and planning at Hunter College in New York City.

In spite of rising nativism, practical constraints and political opposition make it unlikely that the United States can significantly reduce the number of immigrants it accepts. Therefore, the immigration debate should center not on *how many* immigrants to admit, but on *which* immigrants to admit. Rather than discriminating based on family ties, skill levels, or U.S. foreign policy interests, the United States should allow immigration on a "first-come, first-served" basis.

The trouble with the immigration debate of the past year or so is that much of it is simply unreal. Intellectuals have been arguing over abstractions, while the insecurities of ordinary Americans have been inflamed by prejudice and misinformation. Those both for and against immigration behave as if it were politically conceivable that the United States might drastically cut immigration again, as we did in the 1920s, and as if our borders could be effectively sealed if we chose to do so. In spite of resurgent nativism, any proposal to sharply curtail legal immigration would meet massive resistance across the political spectrum—from liberals who see open immigration as a basic ingredient of the universalist American idea to conservatives attached to free markets and open international borders. If it came to a vote in Congress, a bipartisan pro-immigration alliance would emerge even stronger than the one behind NAFTA [North American Free Trade Agreement], using the same arguments (the long-term economic benefits of immigration outweighing its short-term stresses, the politics of fear versus the politics of hope, etc.). Buttressing the argument would be our proven inability to stem illegal immigration, because any reduction in the quota of legal immigrants almost certainly would be offset by an increase in illegal immigration—an unsettling prospect for most Americans, but especially for the nativists.

Peter D. Salins, "Take a Ticket," *The New Republic*, December 27, 1993. Reprinted by permission of *The New Republic*, ©1993, The New Republic, Inc.

So rather than contesting the volume of immigrants, we might re-examine how we actually allocate immigration in a world where the number of potential immigrants vastly exceeds the most generous quota we could tolerate, and how we treat immigrants once they get here. But first, a few facts to reassure ourselves about the benign nature of immigration. To begin with, America is not being inundated with immigrants. While the volume has risen steadily since the national origins quota system was scrapped in 1965, the rate of immigration relative to the nation's base population is far below historic levels. Due in large part to the amnesty of 1.5 million illegal aliens as part of the Immigration Reform and Control Act of 1986 (Simpson-Rodino), the average rate of legal immigration in the 1981 to 1990 period reached a post-Depression high of 3.1 per 1,000 U.S. residents. This rate is below that of every decade from 1830 to 1930, and is about the same as the long-term immigration rate since American independence. Moreover, the percentage of foreign-born in the U.S. population has fallen from 8.8 percent in 1940 to 6.8 percent today.

As important as the volume of immigration is its geography. Most immigrants remain near America's gateways at the perimeter of the country. The greatest number, nearly 40 percent of the total since 1987, live in Southern California, with other large cohorts in New York City, south Florida, Texas and Chicago. Most of the rest can be found in a handful of urban areas on the east and west coasts. Most Americans do not live near immigrants. This suggests either that the new nativism is confined to the peripheral immigrant bastions or that some nativists don't need to meet immigrants to dislike them.

Another critical fact: immigrants have been moving to—and staying in—America's cities, filling a vacuum left by native urban households that have been fleeing to the suburbs for more than forty years. Until a new surge of immigration into New York in the 1980s, the city had been losing population—nearly a million from 1970 to 1980. Since 1980 New York is the only city east of the Mississippi to gain population. Wherever they have settled, immigrants have reclaimed inner-city neighborhoods that had fallen into a state of advanced decay. True, poor blacks and other native minorities moved to these zones of white abandonment first, but at unviably low densities, and with households whose poverty and pathology only exacerbated their devastation.

The debate should be not about how many, but rather who, and how, they should be let into the country.

In spite of their growing presence in American cities, immigrants have not displaced the native minority poor in the labor force. Hypothetically, the low-wage, low-skill work done by the least skilled immigrants in these ethnic enclaves might otherwise have employed native blacks or Puerto Ricans. But most of these jobs didn't exist before the immigrants came, and most native workers would have spurned them even if they had. As a matter of fact, recent studies show that the unemployment rates of blacks living in or near immigrant enclaves actually fell, following the immigrant influx. Immigrant labor also does not appreciably lower native workers' wages very much. A study by Robert LaLonde and Robert Topel estimates that when immigrant participation in a local labor market doubles, the wages of young blacks in general may fall by 4 percent or less, and those of other minorities are unaffected.

How about the indirect economic impact of immigration on state and local government budgets that California's Governor Pete Wilson is so concerned about? All these immigrant children require an education and, at $5,000 per child—thousands more than their parents' local tax contribution—they have filled up the inner-city schools. Here, too, the burden looks greater in the abstract than in reality. Frankly, these inner-city school systems—in New York, Chicago, Miami and L.A.—were dying before the immigrants came. With declining populations, the districts still absorbed a large amount of public funds, without much to show for them. Just as with the cities' dying neighborhoods, the immigrants rescued the schools, not only from bankruptcy, but also irrelevance.

What about that most frightening of the nightmare scenarios promoted by the immigration alarmists: that America will become—God help us—a *nonwhite nation*. Of course, the proper response to this hobgoblin should be: So what? But even those who secretly harbor misgivings about a radical change in the country's racial profile can relax, because the vanishing white majority scare is vastly overblown. The two largest immigrant groups are Hispanic and Asian. Now, Hispanic is not a racial category at all; it's a linguistic one. Even the newer label for this group—Latino—is not racial, it's geographic. Whatever the label, the Latino cohort is very racially mixed, from as white as any Northern European to darker than most native blacks. The vast majority, however, including most Mexicans, have a mixed racial background, and—not that it matters—don't look very different from Americans of Southern European descent, and classify themselves as white in surveys. The same is increasingly the case for Asians.

Who should be let in?

The truth is, the immigration scare does not reflect a genuine problem, it reflects a genuine panic. The panic is brought on by economic dislocation, which is all too easily laid at the door of immigrants. That is not to say there should not be an immigration debate. On the contrary, it is long overdue. The debate should be not about how many, but rather who, and how, they should be let into the country. Categorical preferences built into the current immigration policy exacerbate both the geographic and ethnic concentration of immigrants, adding to the burden of their assimilation, and pouring fuel on the nativist fires. It's time it was overhauled.

The liberalization of immigration legislated in 1965 was supposed to end the Northern European bias of the nativist-inspired national origins quota system of 1925. The reforms certainly succeeded in that respect, changing the source of immigration from Northern Europe to Latin America and Asia. But, at the same time, the preference categories of the current law have perpetuated the root bias of a national origins system, only with a new set of favored nationalities. The largest preference categories under present immigration policy promote "family reunification." This means that once a nationality gains a significant demographic foothold in the United States, it has a vested claim on the immigration quota roughly in proportion to its share of the foreign-born population: exactly the concept that animated the old national origins system. Indeed, the family preferences were written into the 1965 law primarily to reassure the nativists that the national origins idea was not being scrapped entirely. Since the new law's inception, around 70 percent of all legal immigrants have been admitted under one or another family reunification preference category. And with the amnesty provision of the Simpson-Rodino law, the preference has been effectively extended to millions of illegal immigrants as well.

The primary beneficiaries of immigration's family reunification tilt have been Mexicans. Since 1981 more than 30 percent of all legal immigrants to the United States have come from Mexico. The fact that Mexicans account for only 18 percent of all legal immigration since 1965 proves that the national origins bias of family reunification increases over time. Family preferences have also insured that what remains of the pool of legal entrants is dominated by other Latin Americans and Asians from just a few countries: the Philippines, China, Korea and India. The Simpson-Rodino amnesty of 2.5 million illegals, the vast majority of them Mexicans, has further intensified the nationality biases of family reunification, and has been a major factor in provoking a nativist backlash.

Refugee and asylum preferences . . . have been
seriously compromised by our foreign policy biases.

The question we failed to ask in these matters is: Why family? The truth is, the family preference violates the underlying rationale of immigration. The United States has historically welcomed immigrants, to a much greater extent than any other modern society, for a number of reasons. Cynics say it did so because some of its most powerful industries needed cheap labor. Sure, but this need could have been filled by merely admitting "guest workers" as the Europeans do. There has been a deeply idealistic aspect to most Americans' acceptance of immigrants. Americans believe in starting over and giving people with ambition and determination, at home and abroad, the opportunity to do so. Americans also realize, intuitively, that immigrants have the ability to recharge the national batteries, supplying new skills, new perspectives, new cultural attributes, that can make the country a more successful and cosmopolitan nation. It was because the national origins immigration quotas violated these basic precepts that the old system was scrapped in 1965. Well, the current system is coming to violate them even more, with nationality biases greater than those of the old system, and mostly because of the family bias.

The other favored set of foreigners are those admitted under refugee and asylum preferences, who account for 15 percent of all immigrants during the last decade [from the early 1980s to the early 1990s]. Refugee and asylum preferences have a solid justification, given all the repressive regimes in the world, but they have been seriously compromised by our foreign policy biases. When both Nicaragua and El Salvador were in turmoil during the 1980s, Nicaraguans fleeing a Communist dictatorship were accepted as refugees, while Salvadorans fleeing right-wing death squads were not. Likewise, Cubans were admitted as refugees from the time Castro took power, while no dictator is bloody enough for Haitians to be welcomed. And since most Third World autocracies are also poor, every refugee/asylum case involves a judgment call as to whether its motivation is economic or political.

So there are good reasons to change the preference system. How to do it? There are some who would replace the family-based preferences with ones favoring high levels of skill or education, like Canada does. But such a "designer immigration" bias is not only unfair—vesting the privilege of American immigration in precisely those who have been the most privileged in their native lands—it is not even especially helpful to the economy. Our real labor needs—notwithstanding popular perceptions and high unemployment rates among unskilled natives—are at the bottom of the labor market, mainly in services. And the labor market's demand for skilled professionals is amply met by the large number of foreign students who stay and work here after their graduation and by immigrants admitted on other than skill preferences.

A first-come, first-served policy

Why not, instead of unfair family rules and unnecessary skills rules, adopt a policy that effectively makes admission to the United States a matter of "first-come, first-served." Of the roughly 700,000 legal (non-amnesty) immigration slots we make available in a typical year, perhaps 150,000 could be reserved for the spouses or minor children of U.S. residents—a much reduced preference for the reunification of nuclear families—and perhaps 75,000 could be set aside for refugees. The other 475,000 could be available for applicants from any nation on earth. How might such a system work? Subject to an annual global cap, applications for immigration would be reviewed and approved in the order they were received at designated centers in each country. To avoid having the immigrant pool swamped by applicants from the most populous countries (with 40 percent of the world's population, China and India might dominate such a system) perhaps no country's annual quota should exceed some percentage of the total. However it were fleshed out, the objective of such a first-come, first-served concept would be to offer immigration to the most highly motivated candidates, from a maximally diverse set of backgrounds, selected by the fairest and most objective of procedures.

The United States has not made a mistake by admitting millions of immigrants since the law was changed in 1965. Indeed, America's liberal immigration policy is one of our proudest public accomplishments. But America's liberal immigration policy is more likely to find continued acceptance among most Americans and keep the nativists at bay if the immigration preference system is changed to assure a fairer and more nationally diverse pool of immigrants. So let's not turn our backs on one of the most successful American ideas. Let's get it right.

13

U.S. Immigration Policy Should Embody Humane Considerations

Gregory DeFreitas

Gregory DeFreitas teaches economics at Hofstra University in Hempstead, New York, and is the author of Inequality At Work: Hispanics in the U.S. Labor Force.

While immigration is not responsible for America's economic problems, increased immigration could create social and economic stress. Consequently, immigration levels should not be significantly restricted or increased. Rather, U.S. policies should be changed to emphasize humane priorities and to improve living and working conditions both in the United States and abroad. The United States should give preference to genuine political refugees over economic migrants. Moreover, the U.S. government should cease its counterproductive policies toward Third World countries—such as funding repressive regimes and encouraging extreme privatization, which contribute to the social and economic conditions that drive workers to emigrate.

What do rising unemployment, falling wages, soaring budget deficits, and the bombing of New York's World Trade Center [on February 26, 1993] have in common? The answer for more and more politicians and others of late has been: immigrants. Last year's [1993] arrests of alien suspects in the twin towers bombing and the grounding nearby of a ship smuggling almost 300 Chinese refugees [on June 6, 1993] reignited the long-simmering national debate over whether immigration is "out of control."

The debate has been most intense in recession-weary California, home to the largest number of new entrants. In July 1993, Governor Pete Wilson attacked immigrants for "eroding the quality of life for legal residents of California," and launched a campaign to refuse public services to undocumented aliens and to amend the Constitution to deny their U.S.-born children the right to citizenship: Wilson's actions were widely rec-

Gregory DeFreitas, "Fear of Foreigners: Immigrants as Scapegoats for Domestic Woes," *Dollars & Sense*, January/February 1994. Reprinted with permission. *Dollars & Sense* is a progressive economics magazine published six times a year. First-year subscriptions cost $18.95 and may be ordered by writing to *Dollars & Sense*, One Summer St., Somerville, MA 02143.

ognized as ploys to revive his record low popularity ratings before the 1994 election by shifting the blame for his state's problems to a federal issue over which he has little control.

But both of California's Democratic senators quickly followed with their own, if qualified, criticisms of current immigration levels, and President Clinton announced a $173 million proposal to reinforce the border patrol, tighten the asylum process, and introduce a national worker identity card. These politicians have a receptive audience: surveys by *Newsweek* and other publications show that over three-fifths of Americans believe that immigration should be curbed.

The public has three major concerns. First, that the country is "under siege" by unprecedented waves of immigrants. Second, that job-hungry newcomers aggravate U.S. unemployment by competing with the native-born for scarce openings, as well as weakening natives' ability to resist wage cuts. And finally, that many low-skilled migrants are exploiting public programs such as welfare, straining already overburdened state and local budgets.

These fears are largely unfounded. Immigration rates today are lower than at other times in U.S. history; immigrant workers do not harm the bargaining positions of native workers; and immigrants contribute more in federal, state, and local taxes than they use in social services. There are cost pressures on government budgets in localities where immigrants are concentrated, but they could be eased by progressive federal policies.

Although "open borders" would not be a feasible policy, current immigration levels are not a significant cause of U.S. economic problems. Popular anger at immigrants is a misguided response to the nation's prolonged high unemployment levels and declining real incomes.

The measure of immigration

While immigration is now higher than in recent decades, it is not growing as fast as some statistics suggest. Nor are the levels unprecedented compared to other periods of U.S. history.

The United States granted "green cards" (permanent resident immigrant status) to nearly 974,000 people in fiscal year 1992. This was one-third more than the annual average in the 1980s, which was itself two-thirds higher than the 1970s average. And the view is commonplace that massive illegal entry adds many hundreds of thousands more. But the legal migration figures for 1989-92 were inflated by the special amnesty of 2.6 million undocumented aliens under the 1986 Immigration Reform and Control Act (backed by then-President Ronald Reagan and then-Senator Pete Wilson). Excluding them, there were 759,000 new legal immigrants in 1992 and an average of under 600,000 per year in the 1980s.

Immigrants are overwhelmingly drawn by the hope of better jobs, not by U.S. benefits programs.

Although the Immigration and Naturalization Service (INS) once claimed that the number of illegal entrants was between 8 and 12 million, research by Census Bureau and academic demographers in the 1980s put the figure closer to 3 million—about how many eventually sought legalization under the 1986 Immigration Reform and Control Act. Recent INS reports of over 1 million arrests of undocumented aliens per year are invalid, since multiple arrests of repeat border crossers inflate those numbers greatly. In contrast, the Census Bureau estimates that an average of about 200,000 have been entering annually so far in the 1990s.

The relevant measure of immigration levels is the *net* increase in population, after subtracting emigrants leaving the United States. The Census Bureau projects that, adjusting for emigration of 160,000 people a year, the average annual net immigration will be 880,000 in the near future. This is fewer than the number successfully absorbed by the country's much smaller economy in the peak period 1900-1910. At the end of that decade, the foreign born were 14.6% of the U.S. population, compared with only 8% today. The nativists of those years blamed recent (mostly southern and eastern European) immigrants for everything from "racial dilution" to importing Bolshevism to inciting the 1919 steel strike.

Immigrants do not steal jobs

Regardless of the precise number of new immigrants, many Americans are concerned about their impact on the economy. The common belief is that, given the limited number of jobs available, more immigrants mean more competition with native workers, pushing down wages and causing job losses. Some economists say this is particularly true for those occupations in which immigrant workers are concentrated. If immigrants, on average, have relatively low skill levels, then less-skilled native workers, including minorities, could be hit the hardest. Anti-immigration organizations like the Federation for American Immigration Reform (FAIR) have widely publicized a few case studies, like that of Rice University's Donald Huddle on Houston's construction industry, in support of such claims.

But empirical research by a diverse array of economists refutes such arguments. Economists have faulted local studies for deriving misleading conclusions based on partial and static evidence. Huddle simply assumed that the presence of undocumented workers on a job site meant that natives must have been displaced. He ignored a host of other possible adjustments—such as natives moving into higher-pay and status occupations; natives' unwillingness to accept the poor wages and working conditions of certain firms; and immigrant entrepreneurs' formation of new firms in untapped market "niches."

In contrast, studies of the entire labor market of specific cities like Los Angeles and Miami have found that increased immigration had no overall effect on the unemployment of native-born workers. Several national studies covering multiple cities have produced similar results. I looked at 1980 census data on the 79 largest metropolitan areas and found no statistically significant negative effects of immigration on either the wages or employment of native low-skilled workers.

Moreover, other studies show that average skill levels have risen for immigrants from most countries, so that many of them are competing for high- rather than low-skill jobs. This has taken place at the same time that the immigrant share from less-developed countries has grown. A preliminary Census Bureau analysis of 1990 survey data shows that 24% of migrant adults arriving in the 1980s had a college degree, compared with 19% of earlier migrants and 20% of American adults in general.

As with the less-skilled, researchers have found that skilled natives have not lost their jobs or faced lower wages due to recent immigration.

In fact, the only group which may experience adverse effects is the older immigrant population: Some studies suggest a degree of job competition between earlier and recent arrivals.

New immigrants have not worsened the lot of the native born because their arrival has increased not only the supply of workers, but also domestic job growth. Immigrants have above-average self-employment rates, and the new businesses they create mean new jobs, tax revenue, and often new life for marginal and declining urban areas. In addition, they spend their earnings on local consumer goods, cars, and houses, generating multiplier effects that spur more labor demand. And many fill the harshest, low-wage jobs spurned by natives, instead of competing for similar work.

Taxes and benefits

Do immigrants overuse welfare and other social programs and underpay taxes? Two recent, much-publicized reports claim that they do. A 1992 Los Angeles County study alleged that immigrants cost the county $947 million in social services in 1991, but paid county taxes of only $139 million. Another study by Donald Huddle extrapolated from the Los Angeles report to conclude that, nationally, immigrants drained the public treasury of $45 billion.

Subsequent research by Jeffrey Passel and Rebecca Clark of the Urban Institute has shown that the Los Angeles figures overestimated immigrant social service costs by one-third and underestimated their taxes by nearly one-half. Moreover, the Los Angeles report itself estimated that the total taxes (local, state, and federal) paid by these immigrants exceed their total social service costs by $1.8 billion. The discrepancy emerged because most tax revenue flows to Washington, while many of the program costs are borne locally.

> *We should oppose increased admissions of people based solely on their skills.*

Most research has found that immigrants are overwhelmingly drawn by the hope of better jobs, not by U.S. benefits programs. When job prospects dim, many (especially Mexicans) return home.

For refugees without that option, such as the Vietnamese, program usage is more common, at least during the resettlement period. Undocumented aliens are legally barred from most such programs, and seem to largely avoid contact with government agencies out of fear of detection.

Many legal immigrants also think twice about seeking government benefits, since a record of welfare usage can increase their risk of deportation and decrease their ability to sponsor the entry of other relatives. Moreover, since immigrants tend to arrive at young ages, they have less need for many services than do natives, especially the growing number of elderly citizens.

Rapid influxes of immigrants to particular local areas do impose economic costs, since the federal government provides inadequate resettlement assistance to cities and states. About 60% of all new arrivals move to just four states—California, New York, Florida, and Texas—resulting in strains on local school systems, infrastructure, and the environment.

Despite the mounting evidence that immigration is not responsible for our current economic ills, it remains one of the most difficult issues for either the right or the left to reach a consensus on. While the nativist wing of the Republican Party wants sharp cuts in both legal and illegal migration, libertarians propose an "open borders" policy that would allow markets to set supposedly optimal migration and population levels. Many progressives favor reducing immigration in the hope that it will help stem the decline in union organizing and in job and wage prospects. But others on the left espouse open borders as a humanitarian gesture and/or as a means to redistribute income from rich to poor nations.

While individual immigrants and their families usually do raise their living standards by working abroad, exporting workers is a very inefficient approach to Third World economic development. Those with the motivation and resources to emigrate are seldom from the poorest segments of Third World populations, but rather are the semi-skilled and skilled. Their emigration represents a subsidy to the receiving country from the nation that trained them, as well as a loss of valuable talents to their homeland.

Migrants often do send sizeable remittances back home, but research shows that these typically increase income inequality and dependence on consumer imports among migrants' relatives, rather than helping to meet the social investment needs of their home countries. If the same amount of money was bundled in assistance packages from the West to progressive Third World governments, the long-term development benefits would be markedly greater.

Although research shows that current immigration levels do not harm native workers, an "open borders" policy, resulting in much-expanded immigration, might do so. Such a policy would also be likely to cause social and political disruption in the United States. For example, the Census Bureau estimates that even if annual immigration were only to rise to 1.4 million, by the year 2020 this would drive the U.S. population up to 340 million—nearly 90 million more than today. The foreign born would more than double their share of the country's population. History suggests that the more sudden are such large demographic shifts, the more likely they are to fuel racial frictions and a nativist backlash.

A realistic approach

Rather than either highly liberalized or highly restrictive policies, a realistic progressive approach would combine a humanitarian admissions system with adequate protections of labor and living standards both here and abroad. This would require, first, ending the still-strong Cold War bias toward accepting largely economic migrants from Cuba, Indochina, Eastern Europe, and the former Soviet Union. Instead, the United States should give preference to genuine political refugees.

Where massive refugee displacements occur, as in the recent case of Haiti, multinational resettlement efforts should be made. The federal government, which alone controls immigration policy, must provide those states in which new arrivals are concentrated the financial aid they need to expand their services accordingly.

Next, we should oppose increased admissions of people based solely on their skills, a policy built into the 1990 law by pro-business groups. Instead of meeting supposed "skill shortages" by importing people trained elsewhere, the United States should finally commit the resources needed to provide first-class schooling and training for the rising numbers of less-skilled and underemployed Americans. As native workers are preparing to fill skilled openings, any short-term employer needs can be met by selectively granting the one- to two-year temporary visas already used under current law. These visas and the more than 300,000 student visas now granted each year will provide ample opportunity for foreigners seeking direct access to U.S. training. Occupational qualifications might still be one useful criterion for evaluating the large number of applications from relatives of U.S. residents.

The United States has . . . helped to aggravate unemployment in many countries, leading to greater emigration.

So long as unlimited immigration between high- and low-income countries remains an unrealistic prospect, some form of border control will be necessary. But the Immigration and Naturalization Service (INS) is terribly inefficient and understaffed. The INS needs thorough reorganization, as well as better screening, training, and supervision of its agents. This would help to expedite visa application and review processes, and to assure that the increasingly harsh treatment reported among detained undocumented aliens ceases.

Foreign policy measures

To diminish the need of so many Third World workers to emigrate, the United States must end its historic pattern—from Vietnam to the Caribbean to Central America—of itself creating large displaced populations by giving military and economic support to repressive regimes. Recent revelations of CIA support for the opponents of Haiti's elected President, Jean Bertrand Aristide, are only the latest examples of this behavior.

The United States has also helped to aggravate unemployment in many countries, leading to greater emigration, through its influence on the International Monetary Fund's (IMF) policies. The IMF, which controls much of the lending available to Third World nations, has pushed its borrowers to engage in extreme privatization measures, causing untold economic damage. Instead, the United States should lead other rich nations in funding projects that foster sustainable development and job growth in poor countries. This could be partially financed by imposing "social tariffs" on the products of multinational companies whose labor and environmental safeguards are below acceptable levels. As capital becomes ever more mobile, the only way to reduce labor migration is through improving living and working standards in both sending and receiving countries.

The best way to curtail U.S. employers' preferences for the undocumented is to aggressively enforce health, safety, and other workplace labor standards, raise the minimum wage, and change labor laws to encourage greater unionization. This will reduce the competitive advantage of many firms relying on exploited migrants, at the same time that it betters the lot of both native- and legal foreign-born workers.

Immigration today remains essential to the basic humanitarian goals of offering a haven to refugees and reuniting families. It also offers a valuable source of cultural diversity and dynamism for this country. Since most research studies have found that, at least at recent levels, immigration is not responsible for adverse economic trends, efforts to cut immigration should be opposed, as should nativist efforts to widen racial and ethnic divisions. Rather than scapegoating immigrants for the worsening job prospects of so many Americans, we must place the blame where it belongs: on deindustrialization, deunionization, shortsighted corporate responses to global competition, and the government's economic policies of the past decade.

Resources

"Immigrants: How They're Helping the U.S. Economy," *Business Week*, July 13, 1992; *Inequality At Work: Hispanics in the U.S. Labor Force*, Gregory DeFreitas, 1991; Population Projections by Age, Sex, Race and Hispanic Origin: 1992-2050 U.S. Census Bureau, 1992; *The Effects of Immigration on the U.S. Economy and Labor Market*, U.S. Dept. of Labor, Bureau of International Labor Affairs, 1989.

14

U.S. Immigration Policy Should Be Based on Citizenship

Joel Kotkin

Joel Kotkin is a senior fellow at the Progressive Policy Institute, a politically centrist think tank in Washington, D.C.

The two extremist positions on immigration are unacceptable. Immigration opponents, by focusing on the negative short-term consequences of illegal immigration, deny the long-term benefits of legal immigration and naturalization. On the other hand, immigrants' rights advocates, who propose increased social services and civil rights for illegal immigrants, undermine the legitimacy of U.S. laws and institutions, and add fuel to the argument that immigrants are a social and economic burden. Rather than championing group rights, proponents of legal immigration should insist that immigrants assume the responsibilities of assimilation and citizenship.

The bombing of New York's World Trade Center by Arab immigrants, Chinese aliens marooned off our coasts, and perpetual chaos on the Mexican border—images like these are propelling anxiety about immigration to levels not seen since the Red Scare following World War I.

Although the share of foreigners in the U.S. population today is only half of what it was at the turn of the century, support for a cut in immigration levels, according to the Gallup Poll, has grown since 1986 from just under half to roughly two-thirds. This rising tide of nativist sentiment suggests that we need to refocus our immigration policy on its historic mission: the gradual transformation of newcomers into *citizens*.

Nativists defend tough immigration limits by noting, with considerable justification, that they are being imposed throughout the developed world, particularly in Europe, where anti-foreign sentiment is nearing a fever pitch. Yet unlike Europe, our uniqueness is due largely to immigration; more immigrants have come to these shores than to all other countries combined. Immigration is the very thing that makes us, in the words of sociologist Nathan Glazer, "the permanently unfinished country."

Joel Kotkin, "Making Americans." Reprinted with permission from the June/July 1994 issue of *The New Democrat*, the magazine of the Democratic Leadership Council.

At the same time, the rantings of the neo–Know Nothings are being matched decibel for decibel by the disciples of victimization ideology. Too many advocates for immigrants ignore the role of citizenship in American immigration. Fixated on the "rights" of newcomers, they forget that our society has a reasonable expectation that immigrants will, over time, seek to become responsible contributors to the commonweal.

By returning citizenship to the center of immigration policy, we can shift the debate about newcomers beyond strictly humanistic concerns and toward the ultimate assumption by them of both the rights and obligations of Americans. This citizenship-based view of immigration, however, does not suggest that newcomers must shed their cultural, religious, and emotional ties to their past. In multi-racial empires as far back as Alexander's Macedonia and ancient Rome, Jews, Egyptians, and other "outsiders" could retain their cultures and still gain entry to the highest political and economic circles.

Nowhere has citizenship played a more critical role in shaping economic, social, and political life than in the United States. Although roughly half of European immigrants who came here during the late 19th and early 20th centuries returned home, those who remained and became citizens wove themselves into the fabric of America.

We need to refocus our immigration policy on its historic mission: the gradual transformation of newcomers into citizens.

Sadly, friends and foes of immigration alike tend to overlook the critical long-term contribution of legal immigration and naturalization, focusing instead on the short-term economic and social impacts of illegal immigration. This tends to favor anti-immigration groups, whose influence has been greatly magnified by high unemployment and persistent crime problems in such key debarkation points as New York and Los Angeles.

While anti-immigrant groups yammer most often about illegals, this hardly constitutes the fullest extent of their agenda. Led by the influential [Federation] for American Immigration Reform, restrictionist groups have capitalized on frustrations about illegal immigration to advance their own goal of drastically cutting back *legal* immigration from its current level of 800,000 to around 200,000 annually.

Others, notably Pat Buchanan and Peter Brimelow, a senior editor at *Forbes*, argue that new immigration patterns "abandon the bonds of a common ethnicity." They call for both drastic immigration cuts and a renewed emphasis on bringing in skilled immigrants from Europe, whom they deem more culturally compatible with the American "extended family."

Even these restrictions are too moderate for some. For example, a recent report by an Orange County, California, grand jury that focused mainly on problems linked to illegal immigration grabbed headlines by calling for a three-year moratorium on *all* new entrants to the country.

In the process, the grand jury virtually ignored the enormous economic and social contributions of the county's predominately legal and growing immigrant population. For example, Asian and Latino newcomers have become the critical force driving the area's non-defense-related manufacturing economy.

This pattern is even more pronounced in Silicon Valley, where today roughly one in three engineers is an immigrant (most likely an Asian, with large numbers of Russians, Britons, and Israelis thrown into the mix). When asked several years back whether Texas would ever surpass California as a center for high technology, Dallas venture capitalist L.J. Sevin replied: "No, for two reasons: We don't have the Pacific Ocean and enough Asians."

Immigrants are also playing a critical role in key urban regions as owners of technology businesses. In fact, six of the fourteen CEOs on the *Orange County Business Journal*'s list of top manufacturers were born outside the United States, hailing from such countries as Mexico, Pakistan, China, Taiwan, and the former Yugoslavia.

Kingston technologies, the nation's fastest-growing technology company with annual sales of roughly $700 million, was founded in 1988 by Chinese immigrants. Today, it creates jobs for hundreds of people in northeast Orange County, many of them workers at subcontractor firms also owned by immigrants. Its own 300-person work force includes immigrants from at least 20 countries.

"There is a creativity and drive here you won't find in a regular American company," notes Ron Seide, the company's head of marketing and an Ohio native. "There's a lot to be learned from all the different kinds of people here."

Immigrants' entrepreneurial impact extends far beyond the technology field. In Los Angeles County the number of Latino- and Asian-owned businesses, most founded by or serving immigrants, has more than tripled since the early 1980s, a rate far surpassing the groups' growth in population. Statewide, the number of Asian-owned businesses is growing at five times the rate for California businesses in general.

Indeed, according to recent U.S. Census Bureau statistics, Asians and Latinos enjoy far greater economic mobility in California than do either Anglos or African-Americans. And contrary to stereotypes, Latinos boast the *highest* rate of male labor force participation and one of the *lowest* rates of dependence on Aid to Families with Dependent Children of any ethnic group in California. Welfare rates among immigrants are slightly above the national norm, in fact, only because of the high number of refugees receiving AFDC.

Similar patterns can be seen in Chicago, Houston, Miami, New York, and other urban areas. All have retained dynamic entrepreneurial economies while similar cities such as Detroit, St. Louis, and Atlanta that have experienced far less immigration have suffered. Noting the continued growth of such New York areas as Fort Lee, Flushing, and Chinatown, one metropolitan regional economist noted: "There's nothing wrong with New York that a million Chinese couldn't cure."

The Third Worldist approach

These critical economic contributions alone should be enough to make the public pause over drastic cuts in immigration. Liberal advocacy groups, however, have helped keep the issue alive by trying to blur the distinction between legal and illegal immigrants, prospective citizens and temporary sojourners. In fact, by promoting the euphemism "undocumented" over the traditional description "illegal," the advocates seem to be questioning the validity of American law itself.

Advocates' uncompromising defense of "rights" for the undocumented also plays right into the hands of the immigrant-bashers. By seeking to expand illegals' access to virtually all public services, they fuel the restrictionist argument that immigration expands the welfare burden. Similarly, by opposing the deportation of illegals arrested for felonies, they perpetuate the belief that the nation is playing permanent host to a foreign criminal class.

The immigrant-rights lobby and its political allies truly go off the deep end, however, with their calls for the extension of voting rights to non-citizens, the quintessential expression of citizenship. To proponents of the idea—including Julian Nava, a former Los Angeles mayoral candidate and former U.S. ambassador to Mexico, and Leticia Quezada, head of the L.A. school board—enfranchising non-citizens is a simple extension of basic civil rights. Quezada, who is fond of comparing Los Angeles with South Africa, explained her position to *Insight* magazine this way: "At one time only white males could vote. My position is that it's time we cross that line in terms of citizenship."

This "Third Worldist" approach contrasts starkly with that of the old urban Democratic machines and ethnic organizations that included "Americanizing" newcomers in their missions. The approach also enjoys little popular support among both native and naturalized Americans. Three-quarters of Mexican-Americans, two-thirds of Cubans, and four-fifths of Puerto Ricans feel there is too much immigration and are deeply concerned about illegal immigration. According to a 1990 poll by the *San Francisco Chronicle*, the vast majority of Bay Area Chinese, Filipinos, and Latinos think English should be California's official language.

The Third Worldists' call for linguistic rights also seems out of step with the natural proclivities of immigrant children. According to a recent study of census data by sociologists Ruben Rumbaut and Alejandro Portes, more than two-thirds of immigrant children in San Diego and over four-fifths of those in south Florida prefer English to their parents' or any other foreign language; more than 90 percent possess "very high" knowledge of English. At Orange County's Westminster High School, even the Vietnamese Club conducts its meetings in English.

Contrary to the fulminations of the cultural nationalists and Marxists who dominate many advocacy organizations and ethnic-studies departments, most immigrant children want nothing so much as to succeed in capitalist society. The Portes-Rumbaut study of immigrant youths found that three-quarters believe they will attain a college degree or higher, with most looking to assimilate at high levels as professionals or business owners.

Given these realities, the call for "group rights" can only be seen as needlessly bolstering concerns about cultural balkanization and economic dependency expressed by many nativists. In a curious way, the extremists on both sides seem determined to force us to choose between two disagreeable options: an ever-expanding illegal population with virtually unlimited access to public rights and services, and severe restrictions on all immigration.

Supporters of legal immigration must struggle to prevent this from happening since the most likely result would be a massive crackdown on all immigration. To preserve traditional citizen-based immigration, we must face up to the harsh necessity of limiting illegal immigration—due to both its social costs and affront to the legal order—while encouraging the assimilation and citizenship process.

Equally important, advocates of citizenship-based immigration must begin to confront the tougher economic and social consequences of massive migrations. Clearly, some legal immigrants, particularly those from developing countries, lack the educational and entrepreneurial skills to succeed quickly in the United States. Many immigration advocates ignore this reality, acting almost as if the United States has an obligation to run an "affirmative action" policy for the Third World that imposes no expectations on newcomers.

Hopefully, a halting search for a middle ground between the nativists and the advocacy groups has begun. Politicians with strong records in favor of civil and immigrant rights, such as Sen. Dianne Feinstein, D-Calif., have moved to curb the costs of illegal immigration. President Clinton, meanwhile, also stated that getting control of illegal immigration would be a "priority" for his Administration.

We must face up to the harsh necessity of limiting illegal immigration . . . while encouraging the assimilation and citizenship process.

Unlike the advocacy groups, which are largely insulated from the real world by their foundation and corporate grants, Clinton and other political leaders can feel the earth moving beneath them on this issue. They know the people, including most Latinos and Asians, want stronger enforcement along our borders and limited access to public welfare for newcomers.

Yet the ultimate solution to the immigration dilemma lies not in simply responding to public opinion, but in re-examining core issues. This involves looking carefully at the moral, economic, and social benefits of immigration for a society locked in a long-term global struggle for economic and technological pre-eminence.

Immigrants could well prove a critical national resource in this contest. The studies of south Florida and San Diego youngsters found that most study longer and perform somewhat better in school than average. Groups that arrive with high levels of educational achievement—for example, Russians, East Indians, and Filipinos—do particularly well.

In addition, the study of immigrant youths found that many groups such as Indochinese make remarkable progress within a single generation. According to the comparative examination of ninth graders in San Diego, Vietnamese teenagers, nearly all of whose parents were on welfare 20 years ago, now boast the highest grades and greatest commitment to study of any immigrant group.

"No group started out more indigent in modern U.S. history than the Vietnamese," notes Rumbaut, the report's co-author. "But as far as the children are concerned, what is clearly happening is an economic shift toward becoming a well-educated and economically successful population."

Even Hmong children, whose parents are often preliterate and nearly half of whom are on welfare, scored higher in the San Diego sample than Anglos and many other immigrant groups. One reason Indochinese immigrants do so well may be that, like Jews earlier in this century, they come here with little chance or hope of ever returning home. Within a generation, they are almost certain to apply for citizenship; their children, for the most part, have strong incentives to succeed within the mainstream.

In contrast, other immigrant groups, particularly Central Americans and some Caribbeans, often come here with one eye fixed on return to their native countries. This perhaps explains their far lower levels of academic achievement. Viewing themselves more as sojourners than as future Americans, they tend to be slower than other ethnic groups in perfecting their grasp of English, overcoming pre-industrial cultural patterns, or pursuing citizenship.

Although an ambivalent attitude about nationality may be fine for "guest workers," it does little to promote incorporation of immigrants into the general society. In the worst cases, such attitudes foster the creation of separatist movements, youth gangs, and other expressions of alienation.

To some extent, the severe problems afflicting groups such as New York's Dominicans, whose welfare dependency rates now surpass those of Vietnamese, Russian, and Cuban refugees, can also be linked to their exposure to a dysfunctional inner-city milieu. Adding more poor immigrants to the ghettos of New York's Washington Heights, Los Angeles' South-Central and Pico Union, or Miami's Liberty City could simply exacerbate already severe social problems both for immigrant families and host communities.

As a result, we may need to shift our immigration priorities away from politically expedient quotas, particularly for family reunion, which now account for well over two-thirds of all immigrants. For one thing, the emphasis on family reunion often favors the migration of economically inactive elderly persons, as evidenced by the fivefold increase in elderly noncitizen Supplemental Security Income recipients over the past decade. One possible solution: Permit family reunion but only when the sponsoring family accepts financial responsibility for the newcomer's care.

It may also be wise to move toward policies that favor the entrepreneurial and technically skilled migrants critical for our economic development. Although some nativists believe this approach will lead to an influx of white European immigrants, the existing "surplus" of such talent lies largely in East Asia, the Indian subcontinent, and other parts of the developing world. Rather than boost European immigration, it may simply shift the source of newcomers from one set of Third World countries to another.

Similarly, a new immigration policy might also seek ways to screen out those refugees whose ideological orientation, such as extreme Islamic fundamentalism, may prove hostile to American political interests. During the Cold War, we were obliged to take in refugees, notably from Cuba and Indochina, who faced persecution from our communist enemies. Today, such ideological considerations are far less compelling and need to be balanced with a greater concern for long-term national interests.

Ultimately, the debate about immigration cannot simply be about short-run economic or political factors. It must be fixed in a core set of values about citizenship that seeks the creation of a new community based on a shared belief in our Constitution, our institutions, and the renewability of the American dream.

15

It Is Not Necessary to Reduce Immigration to Preserve the Nation

Richard John Neuhaus

Richard John Neuhaus is editor in chief of First Things: A Monthly Journal of Religion and Public Life.

Although American society is a "civic nation" of individuals, it is founded on an Anglo-Saxon, Protestant culture and ethnicity. Critics are wrong, however, to argue that large numbers of recent immigrants from Latin America, Asia, and the Middle East threaten to undermine the civic nation. A greater threat to the nation arises from alienated segments of the native population, such as the urban underclass, civil rights leaders, and members of the cultural elite. Immigration should be controlled, but it does not need to be reduced to preserve the civic nation.

Like many American Jews, Martin Peretz, editor in chief of *The New Republic*, had until now a deep inhibition about ever, ever visiting Germany. But he took the plunge and returns with some instructive observations about that country, and ours. Germans, he suggests, have almost gone overboard to "mortify themselves over anti-Semitism despite Germany having done more to purge this poison than any other country in Europe." He writes admiringly of Germany as Europe's "most responsible collective citizen" in responding to the masses of refugees trekking Westward as a consequence of the turmoils following the collapse of Communism. Although shortly after his visit Berlin put new restrictions on such mass immigration, one doubts that this would change Peretz's respect for the German model as the world tries to cope with changing notions of citizenship and nationhood.

"The advanced countries," Peretz writes, "are now having to choose between being civic nations and ethnic nations, a choice they could elude so long as huge masses of 'others' did not pass through their portals. It was easy to be a civic nation of individuals until new ethnics with new demands for ethnic rights put into question what 'we' meant. This is tinder-box material, especially when ethnic and racial minorities demand

Richard John Neuhaus, "Immigration and the Aliens Among Us," *First Things*, August/September 1993. Reprinted with permission.

cultural and political outcomes that they want to deny to the defining or founding majorities. This has not quite occurred in Germany, at least not yet, but it is happening in the United States."

The distinction between an ethnic and civic nation is important but not as clear-cut as it may at first appear. Civic habits and presuppositions are not unrelated to what we have come to call ethnicity. The civic nation is not simply one of "individuals" but of individuals tied to communities of memory, character, and mutual help. But it is true that, from earlier discussions about the "melting pot" through today's patter about "gorgeous mosaics," most Americans have insisted that the United States has never been an ethnic nation. That claim has frequently tended to overlook the degree to which the "founding and defining" majority in the American project was, at least until fairly recently, Anglo-Saxon and very Protestant. Scholars can dispute whether Anglo-Saxon—or even North European—qualifies as an ethnic group, but nobody moderately familiar with American beginnings doubts that the founders and definers were not, for example, Arab, African, or Japanese.

The synthesis of Puritan religion and the philosophy of John Locke that defined the civic nation presupposed cultural, moral, and even theological assumptions. The Puritan "errand in the wilderness" and sense of Providential mission, as well as the constitutional bid for a *novus ordo seclorum* [a new cycle of the ages], are the product of a singular cultural phenomenon that, somewhat paradoxically, imprinted upon the American mind both the conviction of universal purpose and the conviction of being a people apart. With what might be called the Protestant Descendency of the last century—a decline recently accelerated by new waves of immigration—these constituting convictions are being sorely tested. It is by no means clear that millions of new citizens can easily be educated to embrace the institutions and procedures of the civic nation without reference to the cultural-ethnic history that brought those institutions and procedures into being.

> *The aliens among us are not the recent immigrants but sectors of the population that have . . . become alienated from the American experiment.*

We should be disturbed but not surprised that there is today a rising agitation—mainly on the right but not only on the right—against massive, some say uncontrolled, immigration to the United States. There is little disagreement about the scandal of a great nation not being able to impose discipline upon access to its borders, notably its border with Mexico. But the present and building debate is about much more than that. It is once again becoming respectable to fret in public about the declining birth rate among Americans of native stock (the "founding and defining" part of the population that may soon no longer be a majority). The huge influx of Latin American, Asian, and Middle Eastern immigrants poses, it is argued, a possibly fatal threat to the civic nation, precisely because the civic nation depends upon undergirding habits and presuppositions that are historically and at present inseparable from cultural and ethnic experience. The great truths proclaimed by "We the People" presuppose some notion of the people involved. Are the "alien hordes" who

have no real relationship to that people, aside from envy of their material success and wanting to share in it, capable of internalizing the civic
nation's foundational truths that are inescapably derived from a particu-
larist history of beliefs about, for instance, Nature and Nature's God?

These anxieties about immigration are hardly new, but neither are
they dismissible simply as a replay of the Nativism of the last century. The
Protestant Descendency, a felt threat in the nineteenth century, is now
undeniable reality. The patterns and communities of adhesion that then
made it possible to think of America as a nation have become increasingly
tenuous. It is not unreasonable to worry that Madison, Jefferson, and others are being vindicated in their fear that our civic institutions were not
designed for, and cannot survive, what they called a "vastly extended Republic." However right he was about slavery—and he was undoubtedly
right about slavery—Lincoln may have been wrong in thinking that the
war that effected its abolition could secure a nation "so conceived and so
dedicated." The conception and dedication was the handiwork of the
founding and defining leadership that, even in the 1860s, feared that it
was losing its hold on the nation's future.

Misdirected anxiety

The arguments and agitations about immigration that are now gaining
currency do indeed raise questions about what is meant by "we" and
about the meaning of civic and cultural nationhood. This is "tinder-box
material," but much of the anxiety is, in our view, misdirected. It is possible that the millions of new Americans arriving in recent years will turn
out to be a force alien to and alienating from the American experiment.
But that fear was much more politically potent, and perhaps plausible, in
the late-nineteenth century when the country faced the "invasion of the
great unwashed," composed mainly of Catholics, Jews, Slavs, and others
who had not been part of the founding and defining moment. Such fears
turned out to be unjustified as the nation rightly took pride in its demon-
strated powers of assimilation, in its ability to "Americanize" the newcomers into a population that revivified the founding and defining ideas
of the American enterprise.

The preponderance of evidence today suggests that immigrants continue to be a revivifying force in our national life. Asians in particular
demonstrate an astonishing capacity to enter into the economic and educational dynamics of American opportunity. In polyglot immigrant
communities such as those found in Queens, New York, where peoples
from fifty or more nations live together in remarkable amity, the level of
American patriotism is almost embarrassingly robust. As Linda Chavez
has recently reminded us (*Out of the Barrio*), the largest immigrant group,
the Hispanics, is in fact many distinct groups, almost all of whom enthu-
siastically embrace the chance to enter into the mainstream American experience. (The possible exception being Puerto Ricans, who, by virtue of
their peculiar ties to the United States, have been infected by the mind-
set of being an alienated and victimized minority.)

Admittedly, the story of the present chapter of immigrant history is
still unfolding. It is possible that some of those from the most radically
different religio-cultural background—Muslims come most immediately
to mind—will assertively and collectively dissent from the foundational
beliefs of our constitutional order. But this is highly speculative. Muslims

are still a relatively small immigrant group. Despite higher and much publicized claims to the contrary, there are probably no more than a million Muslim immigrants in America. And to the extent that there is an organized Muslim immigrant community, its leadership is determined to demonstrate that Muslims are good Americans. Witness the still nascent but eager Muslim efforts to develop "dialogue" relationships along the lines of the long-standing Jewish-Christian dialogues.

A serious problem is posed by the aliens among us, but it is not the problem perceived by those who are agitating an anti-immigration agenda. The aliens among us are not the recent immigrants but sectors of the population that have been here for a very long time and have, for many and complex reasons, become alienated from the American experiment. One thinks, for instance, of the urban and mainly black underclass that is dangerously marginalized from the opportunities and responsibilities of the societal mainstream. Their alienation is exacerbated and exploited by a civil rights overclass that persists in preaching the calumny that the American experiment is inherently and incorrigibly racist. It is far from clear that the civil rights leadership really wants black Americans to be full participants in the society. The political alliance between the civil rights establishment and the gay and lesbian movement, for example, seems designed to guarantee that many blacks will continue to think of themselves as marginal, for homosexuals who constitute no more than 2 or 3 percent of the population are the very definition of social marginality.

More influential than the exploited black underclass are the aliens among us who are entrenched in elite positions of cultural leadership, notably in the media, the arts, and academe. In the nineteenth century, the cultural elites had few doubts about their responsibility to "Americanize" the newcomers to these shores. That is not the case today. It is commonly proposed among journalists, writers, academics, and a significant portion of the religious leadership that to be Americanized, to be assimilated into this putatively unjust social order, is to be victimized. The multicultural fevers that have seized upon almost the entirety of the American academy reflect an explicit and rancorous rejection of the core beliefs and institutions of the civic nation and the cultural experience that undergirds it.

If there is "tinder-box material" in problems posed by immigration, the fault lies not with the new immigrants but with members of the "defining and founding" population who have turned themselves into aliens in their own land. There are, however, countervailing forces to those in the societal elites who have abdicated their responsibility to transmit to new Americans the promise and obligations of the citizenship to which they aspire. The Protestant Descendency has been largely a decline of the oldline denominations, and in recent decades it has been at least partially countered by the ascendency of a newly assertive evangelical Protestantism that will no longer accept its exclusion from defining how we conduct business in the public square. These "new" Protestants are really the old Protestants redivivus. They are, for instance, quite prepared to pick up the religio-cultural task implicit in the Puritan perception that this is a covenanted nation devoted to "self-evident truths" about humanity and moral duty.

And there are sixty million Catholics, composed mainly of the descendants of the great unwashed, for whom the American dream has been generally vindicated. Perhaps in a quest for social status, some Catholics have followed the Protestant definers and founders into the wilderness of alienation from the American experience. But the general Catholic pattern gives credence to John Courtney Murray's musings of forty years ago that the day would come when Catholics would have to pick up from oldline Protestants in providing moral and religious legitimation for what he called "the American proposition." Catholics, who bore the stigma and realized the promise of the immigrant experience, are not likely candidates for the new anti-immigration campaign that may now be under way.

Nobody should argue against a more rational control of the flow of immigration to this country. A country that loses control of its borders loses something of its sovereignty and self-respect. But more rational control need not mean reduced immigration. The problem of immigration is posed not by the aliens who are coming but by the aliens who are among us. Americans who understand and affirm our defining and founding moment can confidently welcome and assist the millions who will in the years ahead come to seek their piece of that moment's promise. This will only happen, however, if we recognize that the choice is not between our being a civic nation of disengaged individuals or an ethnic nation of group solidarity. The time is long past when America had the option of being an ethnic nation. The hope is to be a civic nation, a community of communities, held together by the shared affirmation of the original definers and founders that "We hold these truths." Given the generally sorry record of nations trying to cope with the challenge of unity in diversity, America has not done at all badly in the past, and keeping that in mind can help it do even better in the future.

16

Roman Catholics Should Work for Liberal Immigration Policies

Roger Mahony

Roger Mahony has been the Roman Catholic Church's archbishop of Los Angeles, California, since 1985.

Anti-immigrant sentiments expressed by politicians and segments of the public run counter to the teachings of the Roman Catholic Church. Catholic tradition holds that the right to immigrate is more fundamental than the right of nations to control their borders. Moreover, according to Catholic doctrine, immigrants symbolize humanity, and should therefore be treated with compassion, kindness, and respect.

In the letter to the Hebrews, we hear these remarkable words: "Continue to love each other like brothers and sisters, and remember always to welcome strangers, for by doing this, some people have entertained angels without knowing it" (Heb. 13:2).

Today we are witnessing a distressing and growing trend among political leaders, segments of the media and the public at large that capitalizes on prevailing fears and insecurity about the growing number of immigrants in our communities. In today's social climate, we have special reasons to study and ponder the Bible's positive view of strangers, sojourners and aliens. (An earlier statement of mine is still most relevant: "Welcoming the New Immigrants," *Origins*, Jan. 16, 1986.) Our biblical tradition encourages us to encounter the "strangers in our midst"—not with fear and negativity, but with compassion and hopeful expectation. Our social teaching challenges us to embody this sentiment in our personal actions, in our response as a community and in public policy.

It is in this context that I find it necessary to call for both a change in attitude and a change in policy toward the immigrant and immigration. It is imperative that all people of good will clearly understand the danger of this growing negative sentiment and the impact it has on those who are its targets. My reflections are meant for all thoughtful people

Roger Mahony, "You Have Entertained Angels Without Knowing It," *America*, November 27, 1993. Reprinted with permission.

who are sensitive to the "signs of the times" and who genuinely desire to create a community in which all people can join together to realize our collective hopes and dreams.

The sad and dramatic images projected through the media keep in the forefront of our consciousness the desperate needs of our sisters and brothers who have been forced to flee political and economic upheavals in their home countries. Ethnic, racial and social conflicts continue to escalate throughout the world, driving people across international borders. We see this clearly in Bosnia-Herzogovina, the Middle East, the former Soviet Republics, Northern Ireland and South Africa. The people of California are keenly aware of the nature of those conflicts because of the anti-immigrant sentiment that has swept across the state. We have a tremendous opportunity to create solutions that can be signs of hope for other regions searching for just and humane ways to confront these challenges. We have the collective potential to create innovative solutions if there is the political and moral will to do so.

Los Angeles is the premier immigrant city of the United States, a place that David Rieff, in his 1991 book with this title, has called the *Capital of the Third World*. Throughout history, migrations have been extremely beneficial—a source of growth and development. (J. Bruce Nichols, in *The Uneasy Alliance* [1988], explores the positive attitude toward migrations in the history of nations.) Our progress and well-being are directly linked to the ongoing contributions of immigrants. Researchers are pointing out the essential role played by immigration in the work force and in the future of California. Anyone who knows California well understands that immigrants are embracing the work ethic in which Americans justly take pride.

Nevertheless, attitudes of suspicion, fear and hatred toward newcomers are on the rise. Rather than recognizing the creative potential of new immigrants, some political leaders have chosen to exploit the most defenseless in our society to divert attention from our unwillingness or inability to confront the more complex causes of economic stagnation, poverty and crime.

The history of the United States is full of instances in which immigrants have been made the scapegoats for social and economic problems. In choosing to exploit the anti-immigrant sentiment, political leaders have played upon some of the more enduring evils in society: selfishness, racism and deeply ingrained cultural prejudices.

In Los Angeles, we have a particular self-interest in addressing these concerns. We are a microcosm of the global community's racial, cultural and ethnic diversity. Most of the world' s languages, cultures and races converge here.

What should be our response to the challenges of immigration? The Catholic tradition proposes certain moral and ethical principles that should guide a reasonable analysis of the issues and the development of fair and just solutions. The rights of immigrants are a theme of extraordinary importance in Catholic social teaching and follow from the basic principles of this teaching, which affirm human life and human dignity. (The most authoritative statements of Catholic social teaching on immigration are Pius XII's 1952 apostolic constitution *Exsul Familia*, John XXIII's 1963 encyclical *Pacem in Terris*, Paul VI's 1971 apostolic letter *Octogesima Adveniens*, the 1969 Instruction from the Vatican's Congregation for Bishops on "The Pastoral Care of People Who Migrate," and the National Conference of Catholic Bishops' 1976 "Resolution on the Pastoral

Concern of the Church for People on the Move.") The right of persons to enjoy and share in the benefits of the earth is an integral part of that teaching. The right to move across borders to escape political persecution or in search of economic survival is explicitly part of that tradition.

Catholic social teaching takes what many view to be a countercultural position on this matter and insists that the right to immigrate is more fundamental than that of nations to control their borders. Yet these principles are difficult to embrace amid deep economic recession and in a time when political motives take precedence.

In confronting the challenge of immigration today, one must sift through the rhetoric fully to understand and analyze the issues and develop policy that respects the rights and dignity of all.

The positive effects of immigration

Over the years, many reports have revealed the *positive* effect of immigration upon the U.S. economy. The research of many respected scholars has documented the astonishing efficiency, productivity and reliability of our immigrant workers—documented or undocumented. There is respected and credible research that documents the positive effect immigration has on our communities and economy. (Researchers at both the Rand Corporation in Santa Monica, California, and the Center for U.S.-Mexico Studies at the University of California in San Diego have produced a number of scholarly works on almost every area of immigration policy. Their findings [often contradicting the negative views on immigration] are regularly overlooked by both political leaders and the media.)

We know, for example, that undocumented immigrants pay more in taxes than they receive in social services. *Business Week* magazine stated in its July 13, 1992, cover story: "Even immigrants with less education are contributing to the economy as workers, consumers, business owners and taxpayers. Some 11 million immigrants are working, and they earn at least $240 billion a year, paying more than $90 billion in taxes. That's a lot more than the estimated $5 billion immigrants receive in welfare."

The right to immigrate is more fundamental than that of nations to control their borders.

We know that the United States and other developed countries are not bearing the major part of the burden of receiving immigrants and refugees. In fact, the vast majority of immigrants and refugees are found in underdeveloped countries of Africa and Asia. This was noted by the Vatican's Third International Congress on the Pastoral Care of Migrants and Refugees, 1991.

We also know that nothing is gained by denying citizenship and access to education to the children of undocumented workers. On the contrary, the human potential of these dynamic new Americans will be lost. Our society will not be improved by creating an even larger under-class deprived of education.

Nothing will be gained by denying undocumented workers and their families access to medical care. Common sense and human decency suggest that we should do everything possible to assure the health of all those who reside in our cities and who perform the work and services that keep our communities in operation. Who, for example, performs the most basic tasks of planting and harvesting and of preparing and serving our food? Are they not in great part the immigrant population? To deny them basic medical care—emergency or preventive—is exceedingly short-sighted. The health of our entire society is affected by the health of these workers regardless of their immigration status.

Indeed, the long-range prosperity of our nation, and especially that of California, depends upon our ability to promote the rights of workers who cross our borders and who serve as a mainstay and support to our economy (see David Hayes-Bautista, W. Schink and J. Chapa, *Burden of Support* [1988]).

Love the stranger

For Catholics, the debate about immigration is derived from a tradition informed by Scripture, papal documents and statements and pastoral letters of our bishops. (For a summary of the major points in Catholic social teaching regarding immigrants see Drew Christiansen, S.J., "Sacrament of Unity: Ethical Issues on Pastoral Care of Migrants and Refugees," in *Today's Immigrant and Refugees* [U.S. Catholic Conference Publications, 1988].) Within this tradition, care for aliens and strangers is one of the most ancient moral imperatives. The Book of Exodus instructs us in these words:

> "You shall not oppress an alien. You well know how it feels to be
> an alien since you were once aliens yourselves in the land of Egypt"
> (Ex. 23:9).

The God we have come to know in Jesus Christ identified closely with our humanity. Sacred Scripture sees the stranger, alien and sojourner as the symbol of the human person in the quest to realize his or her full potential. When we respond kindly to the strangers in our midst, when we honor their humanity, respect their ways and meet their needs, we are doing God's work. Each encounter with the stranger is an opportunity to encounter God anew.

The command to love the stranger occurs nearly three dozen times in the first five books of the Bible. In the Hebrew Scriptures, it is surpassed in its frequency only by the command to adore, love and revere God and God alone (see W. Gunther Plaut, "The Force of the Biblical Word," *Compass*, May/June 1993).

Each encounter with the stranger is an opportunity to encounter God anew.

But the witness of Scripture goes beyond that. The passage from Hebrews quoted at the beginning of this statement reminds us that the immigrant in our midst is an "angel"—a messenger from God. This messenger speaks to our common humanity and destiny—our hopes and dreams that can cross culture, language, race, social class or national heritage.

The stranger in our midst reminds us that the social purpose of economic wealth is not what it achieves for the individual, but how it promotes the common good of society. While each and every human being has a right to private property, to a decent standard of living, we have a responsibility to share, as Pope John Paul II has reminded us, not only "from our abundance, but also from our very substance."

The hearts of Christians whose lives are centered on God cannot help but see Jesus in today's immigrants. Catholics recall the words of Jesus Christ addressed to those who would be His disciples: "I was a stranger and you took me in" (Matt. 25:35). We remind ourselves that the basic characteristic of Christ's true followers is hospitality: "See how they love one another!" The proof of our hospitality is measured not by its exercise when the arrival of strangers is convenient, but precisely when it is inconvenient. In our parishes we must strive to enflesh this effective love by truly serving all, by providing ministries suitable for all racial and cultural groups that make up our worshiping communities.

Much is at stake in the way we respond to the immigrants today. I urge all of you to resist the temptation to join in the mean-spirited scapegoating that is becoming contagious. Our faith-tradition calls us not to follow the lead of those who fan the flames of intolerance.

I encourage you to remember the words from the Third Letter of John: "My friends, you have done faithful work in looking after these brothers, even though they were complete strangers to you" (v. 5). Let these sentiments be our guide as we strive to build up our community.

Immigration for us is not and never will be a problem as much as a great opportunity to embrace fellow human beings with that self-giving and sacrificial love that is the cornerstone of lasting justice and peace.

In Catholic history, the monks modeled that hospitality in their monasteries in the simple refrain: *Venit hospes, venit Christus*—"In the stranger we encounter Christ." Current events demand that we renew our conviction to love and respect strangers and immigrants. In this way, we support all our brothers and sisters in their often heroic quest for a fuller and more abundant life.

In the spirit of Jesus Christ, let us rise above rhetoric and ill will and affirm once again our conviction that the world and its blessings are meant for all of God's children. Let us never exclude anyone from the banquet of life. For it is in welcoming immigrants to our table that we will, in turn, receive abundant blessings.

17

The U.S. Should Not Make Immigrants Scapegoats

Elizabeth Martinez

Elizabeth Martinez is a contributor to Z Magazine, *a left-leaning political magazine published in Boston, Massachusetts.*

Immigrants are increasingly being made scapegoats for social and economics problems in the United States and around the world. In order to create divisions among minorities, racists are blaming immigrants for taking jobs from U.S. workers and draining public resources. Moreover, politicians are joining the immigrant-bashing trend in order to boost their popularity. This attack on immigrants calls for a new civil rights movement that includes immigrant and refugee rights.

Time to face some troublesome facts. In Los Angeles during the 1992 uprising many longtime Mexican American residents said, "We're not the ones rioting, it's those immigrants"—meaning Mexicans and Central Americans. At a San Francisco rally marking the 30th anniversary of the March on Washington in August 1993, Dolores Huerta was speaking. A middle-aged African American woman stood and screamed angrily at Huerta, "Go back to Mexico! We need our jobs!"

Incidents like these—and there are many more—leave us with certain questions: will African Americans be made the shock troops of an ugly campaign by racist whites to scapegoat immigrants for the social ills devastating Black and other poor communities? Will established Latino residents forget where they came from and fail to see the racist, classist divisiveness in today's immigrant-bashing? Shall we all remain blind to the need for solidarity among African Americans and Caribbean Blacks, Arab Americans, Asian Pacific Americans, and Latinos—not to mention progressive whites—in combating today's international attack on immigrants?

Imperatively the times call for understanding what the hell is going on and why. Three questions confront us, as formulated by a homeboy friend the other night: "Who is the gun pointed at? Why is the gun being pointed? What is the gun?"

From the U.S. to Germany to Australia, anti-immigrant actions and policies have escalated in often deadly fashion during recent years. In the

Elizabeth Martinez, "Scapegoating Immigrants," *Z Magazine*, December 1993. Reprinted with permission.

United States, President Bill Clinton wasted little time breaking his campaign promise to end George Bush's inhuman policy toward Haitian refugees. Under Bush and Clinton some 40,000 Haitians have been summarily returned to a military-police dictatorship of unbridled brutality where they would be lucky to escape immediate death. Surely 1993's award for racist immigration policy should go to the U.S., whose officials were sending unarmed Haitian refugees back to Haiti in October 1993 even as other officials pulled armed U.S. forces out, saying Haiti was just too dangerous.

Clinton's action also gave the green light to the right wing's anti-immigrant agenda. His own proposals are aimed at tighter Border Patrol control and a speedup in reviewing asylum requests that could send people to their deaths faster.

In California, government officials have generated a tidal wave of anti-immigrant laws or programs. Governor Pete Wilson led the way with a stream of outrageous proposals, among them denying citizenship to children born in the U.S. of undocumented parents. He got four passed in October 1993 which include a ban on giving driver's licenses to the undocumented, requiring state and local agencies providing job training or placement to verify a person's being a legal resident, and increasing penalties against getting Medi-Cal benefits "fraudulently" or helping others to do so.

Not to be outshone by a Republican, California's two new Democratic women Senators offered their own measures. Even the erstwhile liberal Senator Barbara Boxer urged sending the National Guard to defend the U.S.-Mexico border against my relatives. Some "reformist" politicians like Representative Romano Mazzoli advocate stricter enforcement of employer sanctions. At the heart of the 1986 Immigration Reform and Control Act, these sanctions provided for penalties against those who knowingly hire the undocumented; the sanctions haven't worked but they have encouraged discrimination against anyone who looks or sounds "foreign." As for the Hispanic Congressional Caucus, it has taken a mix of positions.

The attack on immigrants is usually racist.

The North American Free Trade Agreement (NAFTA) also sparks anti-foreign, anti-immigrant sentiment. NAFTA negotiations never address the civil and labor rights of immigrants—only Mexico's responsibilities to stop northbound traffic. An anti-immigrant attitude prevails in the debate over NAFTA, the main issue being whether NAFTA will increase or diminish immigration from Mexico.

California, where 40 percent of those who immigrate to the U.S. settle, has repeatedly seen bombings and other violent attacks on Asian and Latino immigrants or their advocates by ultra-rightists. One image speaks to all these actions. Irma Muñoz, a 20-year-old woman who immigrated from Mexico recently, became a successful engineering student at the University of California, Davis, and began working publicly as an intern for a state legislator advocating less reactionary immigration policies. In April 1993 two white male students at UC Davis punched her, cut her hair, and scrawled on her arms and her back with a black magic marker

"Wetback" and "Go home you illegal." If she told anyone about the attack, they warned, she would be killed along with "your wetback friends" like the legislator.

In Texas, where the second largest immigration occurs, the spectacular "Operation Blockade" went up in September 1993. A Border Patrol inspiration, it put 650 armed agents in a 20-mile-long line facing the Juarez-El Paso border for 24 hours a day, supposedly to prevent "illegals" entering from Mexico—but of course they harassed those with papers too. Overtime costs quickly ran up to $300,000 and anybody could walk around either end of the 20-mile line, but no matter, at this writing the operation continues and will also be replicated in the San Diego area. Somebody fretted that the word "blockade" implies an act of war so the San Diego operation is called "Enhanced Enforcement Strategy." That does sound nicer.

New York, the third main destination of immigrants, saw a tidal wave of anti-immigrant (particularly anti-Arab and anti-Muslim) hatred after the World Trade Center bombing. A September 1993 poll of 1,203 New Yorkers reported "startlingly negative attitudes on recent immigration in a city renowned for its international character." More than 63 percent said the number of recent immigrants was too high and more than two-thirds said immigrants had made New York a worse place to live. As for "illegal" immigrants, 55 percent saw them as a serious terrorist threat and 82 percent of the U.S.-born said they believed tighter controls over immigration could have prevented the World Trade Center bombing.

Add to such hysteria the racist depiction of U.S. shores being assaulted by boatloads of Chinese refugees. Incidents also occur in scattered locales like Fall River, Massachusetts, where 12 white men murdered a Cambodian American and severely beat his friend on August 14, 1993, while racially taunting both. Or the University of Nevada in Las Vegas, where an India-American student died after being set on fire by two men—one white, one African American—who said they didn't want any more foreign students on campus.

Elsewhere in the world: In Germany police reported 2,285 acts of rightist violence in 1992, mostly against foreigners and including seven murders. On May 29, 1993, came the neo-Nazi firebomb killing of five Turks—three young girls and two women—along with other violent attacks on Turkish refugee hostels, homes, and restaurants. A German clerk in a Berlin store falsely accused a Turkish resident of stealing; when the woman's daughter protested, the clerk said "We got rid of 6 million Jews, we'll get rid of you too." Chancellor Helmut Kohl refused to attend a memorial service for the firebombing victims and threatened Turks who might defend themselves. (Of Germany's 1.8 million Turks, many went there 30 years ago invited as guest workers; many were born in Germany.) The German parliament passed a law, which required changing the German constitution, that blocks most applicants for political asylum.

• In France attacks on North Africans have been common, with citizens complaining that Third World immigration "is changing the French way of life." In June 1993 France's National Assembly overwhelmingly approved a new law authorizing police to carry out random identity checks to clamp down on undocumented immigrants.

• In Italy a group of North African immigrant workers were beaten and stabbed by 20 Nazi-skinheads in February 1992.

• In spring 1993 Spain was reported to be increasingly xenophobic toward immigrants from Africa, who numbered 264,000 in Barcelona alone, as well as from South America. An African immigrant in Madrid was murdered in an officially recognized hate crime. An appalling traffic bringing workers from North Africa to Spain by boat has led to 1000 deaths by drowning in the last five years [from 1988 to 1993], 300 in 1992 alone. Apparently nobody cares, again we find the zero value put on the life of a poor black person.

• In Hungary, with 50,000 refugees from the war in the Balkans, Gypsies have been a favorite target. One Gypsy was beaten to death on November 6, 1993, by skinheads.

• Britain sees constant attacks on "blacks" (which includes Indians and Pakistanis). One in three Britons does not want Arabs or Pakistanis as neighbors and two of three said in an October 1993 poll that they don't want to live near Gypsies.

•In Holland middle-class white flight from the schools increases as the immigrant population rises.

•Switzerland's 1991 elections showed rising animosity to immigration when the leader of a rightist party scored big election gains.

• Australia began enacting tough policies in 1992 to deal with an immigration "problem" that critics say does not really exist. And, in an ultimate irony for white folks, we find that immigrants from the Caucasus—yes, Caucasians—who have moved to Moscow since the Soviet Union disintegrated are resented, harassed and attacked as "blacks."

Immigrants have always been a favorite whipping boy and recruitment ploy for rightist forces.

Three chilling commonalities surface in this geographic mix. First, in almost every country the anti-immigrant attack coincides with and nurtures a rapid growth of neo-Nazi and far-right groups. But the New Right is not a fringe creature; it includes "respectable" reactionary politicians, with a number of them winning office on an anti-immigrant platform.

Second, many liberals join reactionary forces in scapegoating immigrants. Some major environmental organizations have formed an anti-immigration alliance and are loudly demanding curbs on immigration for its supposed ecological damage and excess population ("immigrant women have high fertility rates"). It seems that 2-4 percent of the U.S. population causes every evil from pollution to traffic jams.

Third, the attack on immigrants is usually racist (and often anti-Muslim). Paris's conservative mayor Jacques Chirac minced no words: they even have "smells" of their own, he said about immigrants. In the U.S. the very word "immigrant" means people of color in most people's minds; forget the many Europeans.

Why is the gun being pointed?

Immigrant-bashing and persecution embody a ruling class tactic going back centuries that blames "outsiders" for a society's woes. Today's message is: "Don't blame corporate interests, don't blame the Savings & Loan banks, don't blame the government or elected officials, do blame immigrants!"

"Operation Scapegoat" calls for the U.S.-born to see immigrants as individuals who have freely chosen to leave their homes and cultures, and not to see that most people migrate under the pressure of political, economic or social forces. Similarly the receiving country is seen as a passive victim of invading hordes, when in fact its policies may well "pull" migrants in various ways. The U.S. sent $6 billion in aid to El Salvador's government during the 1980s to crush the popular insurgency. Almost 500,000 destitute, frightened Salvadorans moved to Los Angeles, mostly during the 1980s. Could there be a connection?

Foreign policy, including warfare, is one answer to why people move across borders. Other politico-military reasons would be ethnic conflict, civil strife, and persecution. These have had devastating impact in recent years: the massive dislocation of people in Iraq and Kuwait caused by the Gulf War, the aftermath of the Berlin Wall's collapse, and effects of the disintegration of Yugoslavia and the Soviet Union.

The economic reasons for migration are no simple matter but we surely need to look at immigration in relation to global economic trends today. For centuries pressure from the failure of domestic structures to provide basic employment and subsistence has created economic refugees. We can see the effects of contemporary economic restructuring, intended by capitalists to restore their profit rates and to hell with millions of skilled steel workers, auto workers, and others. Arturo Santamaria Gomez, the Mexican professor and author, writes of how globalization has caused a deepening U.S. dependence on the Mexican immigrant work force, for example. "Globalization puts a competitive premium on pools of low-paid, 'flexible,' vulnerable workers," he said in a *Nation* article (October 25, 1993). Mexican and other migrant labor—especially when undocumented—is key to restructuring the U.S. economy.

Historically that labor carries great advantages for the capitalist. It is vulnerable, especially if undocumented, and totally disenfranchised. Here is the most basic function of the border: as a mechanism for defining and maintaining control over labor by the possession or lack of "legal" status. History is packed with experiences of deportation just when an undocumented worker was due to be paid or when workers began to organize for their rights; of low wages and terrible working conditions accepted because the alternative was deportation. Such crippling controls make the undocumented worker a very special kind of wage slave, more enslaved than waged.

But the growth of global economic integration involves more than cheap labor, as immigrant rights activist Maria Jimenez tells us. Why does the *Wall Street Journal* call for a totally open border, even as other voices from center to right demand tighter control? It seems possible the *Journal* understands that today countries belong to an inter-dependent collectivity shaped by global trends. That it questions the role of borders in an era of galloping, global economic integration. Why try to regulate immigration with border control at a time of energetic efforts to open up national economies and create trading blocs like NAFTA?

Saskia Sassen, of Columbia University, a longtime expert on immigration issues, has written about such contradictions. She points out, for example, the way overseas operations of firms have a migration impact. We can conclude, people are moved when investment moves. The real migrant is capital.

Instead of considering such realities, we are barraged with a repertory of hostile myths about immigrants. We hear regularly two key myths.

(1) "Immigrants are taking away jobs." In fact, in the U.S. the Rand

Corporation, the Urban Institute and the Heritage Foundation—hardly dens of leftism—all concluded in various studies that immigrants do not take jobs from native workers and depress wages. *Newsweek* recently reported (and I would agree, from random observation of janitorial and other service work in a few cities) that during times of high unemployment there may be temporary displacement in some job sectors. But even if that happens, new jobs are soon created by the presence of immigrants with their needs for basic goods and services. This temporary displacement is numerically very small. Immigrants mostly work in jobs in highly exploitative sectors like the garment industry, as nannies, or in the fields, with the legalized working 2-5 hours more per day than the general population.

(2) "Immigrants use services but don't pay for them, and thus they drain local and state resources." But again numerous studies show the opposite: immigrants, including the undocumented, pay more in taxes than the cost of the services they use. *Business Week* (of July 13, 1992) reported that immigrants pay $90 billion in taxes each year, while receiving $5 billion in services. (This truth is masked by the fact that much of the tax money goes to the federal government, not the state providing the services.) Also, immigrants use fewer services than the native-born; for the undocumented, always fearful of capture and deportation, the percentage is tiny. The director of the National Immigration Forum says less than 1 percent of newly legalized immigrants received general assistance in 1987-88 and less than half a percent obtained food stamps and AFDC [Aid to Families with Dependent Children]. As for social security taxes, since most immigrants are young they will pay a disproportionate amount of tax for an increasingly aging population.

We need to [define] . . . immigrant and refugee rights as a civil rights issue.

The myths are intended to prove that the very real deprivation experienced today by the U.S.-born should be blamed on immigrants—that largely impoverished 2-4 percent of the population. In California, whose economic problems obviously rise from such setbacks as failed new industries and severe cuts in tax revenue under Prop. 13, this scapegoating seems ludicrous. Instead of swallowing it we should all protest the real causes of the crisis and immigrants should be demanding: No taxation without representation.

Politics is the first, obvious place to find the reasons for those myths. Governor Pete Wilson's approval rating rose seven points soon after his "get tough on immigrants" campaign warmed up. Immigrants have always been a favorite whipping boy and recruitment ploy for rightist forces. Such politics echo the anti-social services, anti-labor shift that has swamped much of the world over the last two decades.

A key part of this shift is the intensification of racism, and racism plays a key role in immigrant-bashing—so often that it's sometimes hard to separate one from the other. In France Jean-Marie LePen's rightist National Front Party has grown steadily for several years on a platform that would cut off immigration specifically of Arabs and Africans.

In the long run, universally humane treatment of immigrants and refugees requires global changes in today's economic policies and the supra-national agencies like the World Bank or GATT [General Agreement on Tariffs and Trade] who determine them. Meanwhile, we must deal urgently with the short run. That calls for two related kinds of action: building a new civil rights movement that includes immigrant and refugee rights, and combating forces that pit people of color or workers against each other by scapegoating immigrants.

On the first front we need to begin by defining immigrant and refugee rights as a civil rights issue around which all must unite. We need a new civil rights movement that recognizes immigrants are usually non-white and are made vulnerable to exploitation and abuse because they lack citizenship and knowledge of English. At the top of our civil rights list is getting the Border Patrol under some control. We need procedures, starting with H.R. 2119, the Immigration Enforcement Review Commission, to investigate complaints about this autonomous agency—the largest police department in the U.S., guilty of rape and murder of defenseless immigrant women and men, almost all Mexican or Central American.

Nothing is more difficult than combating the divisiveness that has pitted people of color against each other. The mass media, right-wing organizations, politicians, and normally progressive voices have established a climate where 63 percent of 500 Latinos polled in California in 1993 thought enforcing employer sanctions was the best way to curb illegal immigration and 73 percent of African Americans believe immigrants are taking their jobs, according to a Harris poll. The right-wing Federation for American Immigration Reform, FAIR, ran radio spots targeting black communities that blamed the problems there on those foreign hordes coming across the border. In a more subtle but equally venal way, TV gives us an automobile commercial in which an African American salesperson says: "Go see *Rising Sun*, then you'll know why you have to buy your car from me."

School children learn racist anti-immigrant epithets heard from parents or the media. To hear a Chicano kid sneer "Mexican" at a day laborer on the street corner is cause to grieve mightily. To hear African American children holler "wetback" at recently immigrated Latino kids who speak too little English for self-defense is also grievous. To hear Latinos object to protests about the bombing of an Asian rights center because "those people didn't have it hard like us" is sad indeed.

We need to set aside narrow, reactionary nationalisms that tell us to care only about our own. We need to welcome and encourage voices that try to expose the scapegoating, like that of Joe Williams III, an African American writing in the *Los Angeles Sentinel* September 9, 1993. Williams compared the current attacks on the undocumented to the harassment of blacks during the 1950s-1960s, when many moved north or west as southern agriculture declined. "They were accused of taking the jobs of the white man. They were accused [by whites] of undermining the salaries of union workers." But it's even worse today, Williams concludes, because mainstream politicians as well as segments of the black and Latino communities join the attacks. About Latino immigrants "We must realize that California and four other states were . . . part of Mexico," he says.

A new civil rights movement should not deny that class differences exist among immigrants, but those don't justify the current denial of civil/human rights across the board. A word must also be said to organized labor: it's time to reject that racist, elitist attitude toward immigrant workers, including the undocumented. Unions need to recognize the courageous determination of workers today like the Los Angeles dry-wallers—almost all Latinos—or the San Antonio garment workers' organization Fuerza Unida—almost all Latinas. It could do much to revive the U.S. labor movement. Civil rights, human rights, labor rights: all are needed.

We are left with a chilling question of our time: Will we unite to fight the divisive scapegoating of immigrants? At the very least that attack will move U.S. society still farther to the right. At worst, it can usher in neo-fascist tendencies.

The immigrant and refugee rights struggle points to our need for a whole new world view. Does anybody really think the way to deal with an estimated one million migrants wandering the planet today is by locking some doors? There is no way that 19th century nationalism can be useful. It is profoundly backward to go on seeing countries primarily as bordered nation-states which can resolve issues like immigration policy unilaterally. *No Hay Fronteras.*

18

Ethnic Cleansing by Attacks on Immigrants Must Be Stopped

La Resistencia

La Resistencia is an organization that combats restrictions on immigration and violations of immigrants' civil and human rights. It opposes aggressive immigration control efforts, the denial of education and social services for immigrants, and popular anti-immigrant sentiments.

With its harsh policies—and calls for even stronger measures—the U.S. government is waging a war on immigrants. Immigrants are falsely blamed for burdening the American economy, but the truth is that U.S. policies oppress immigrants. Because immigrants are denied civil and human rights, they are abused by the Border Patrol and exploited by U.S. employers. Moreover, U.S. policies create the economic and political conditions that push immigrants from their home countries in the first place. The government must be opposed in its attack on immigrants.

On August 10th [1993], California Governor Pete Wilson sent an open letter to President Bill Clinton asking the question, *"Why does the U.S. Government continue to reward illegal immigration . . . at such costs to the American people?"*

What *rewards* is Wilson talking about? The *reward* of being hounded and hunted by La Migra [Border Patrol]—the U.S. Gestapo—that daily carries out beatings and even murders immigrants with impunity? The *reward* of being forced to live in the shadows of society, deprived of the legal right to work? The *reward* of living in overcrowded dilapidated fire traps? The *reward* of having to work in the most dangerous and physically draining jobs for slave wages?

The fact is this: Wilson's letter and his action plan are nothing less than a call for ethnic cleansing—U.S. style! His proposals aim to create a permanent subclass of "non-persons" without citizenship, without health care, without education—and subject to super exploitation and racist discrimination with absolutely no legal recourse. These proposals echo Nazi Germany's anti-Jewish Nuremburg Laws of the 1930's!

La Resistencia, "Attacks on Immigrants Are Nothing Less than a Call for Ethnic Cleansing—U.S. Style!" A flyer published by La Resistencia, Houston, Texas. Reprinted with permission.

Wilson's proposals are part of the U.S. Government's War On Immigrants. This war is being directed from the *top levels* of government with President Clinton picking up where George Bush left off. *Clinton* has continued the kidnapping of Haitian and Chinese refugees on the high seas, "repatriating" them back to the poverty and political repression from which they fled. *Clinton* is adding more Border Patrol agents, increasing the militarization of the border and is pushing laws to severely restrict a person's right to political asylum.

Gov. Wilson's letter is a lesson in scapegoating of the ugliest and most mean-spirited style. Pierce the veil of Wilson's anti-immigrant demagoguery, his lies and statistical distortions, and his hateful agenda gets clearer and more disgusting.

> *Immigrants wrecking the economy?* According to an L.A. County study cited in an *L.A. Times* article (8/13/93) "... immigrants in the county generated $4.3 billion in taxes to all levels of government in 1991 & 1992. Health, social and justice-related services provided to them, as well as to the children of illegal immigrants, amounted to $947 million, and county school districts spent another $1.5 billion. The net impact: a positive contribution of $1.85 billion." It is an outright lie to claim that immigrants take more out of the system than they put in.

> *Immigrants responsible for monumental health care costs?* Studies by the General Accounting Office of Congress as well as academics like Leo Chavez of University of California, Irvine, have found that Latino people, with and without papers, have the lowest level of health care of any population group in the U.S. Imagine the conditions for people deprived of any health care at all!

> *Immigrants filling the jails?* Is it any wonder, when the U.S. has the highest incarceration rate of any nation in the world? The U.S. is pushing 1 million people in prison! For the past decade the government has waged a "War On Drugs" and a "War On Gangs" against people of color, including immigrants. A whole section of Black and Latino youth have been criminalized for the color of their skin, the clothes they wear, and where they live. For the U.S. government to complain about immigrants filling their jails is the equivalent of Hitler complaining that the Jews were filling up his concentration camps!

The government at all levels has tried to make the existence of the undocumented a criminal act. In 1986, the passage of IRCA (Immigration Reform and Control Act) made it illegal for millions of people in this country to work. The Employer Sanctions provisions of IRCA, with the threat of heavy fines against companies who hired undocumented workers, called on employers to turn over undocumented immigrants to the INS [Immigration and Naturalization Service]. It turned millions of employers into assistant INS agents.

These actions by the U.S. Government have forced thousands of people into the underground economy just to survive. It has forced hundreds of thousands to work the most back-breaking dangerous jobs, without health care, without safety regulations and at sub minimum wages. It is the height of hypocrisy for this government to call for a clampdown on immigrants when the U.S. economy has been propped up by the ruthless exploitation of the undocumented for so many years!

Wilson's letter turns reality on its head by portraying immigrants as eco-

nomic opportunists sucking our country dry. The reality is the *U.S. Government* has stripped and sucked dry the resources and economies from which these people have fled. The *U.S. Government* not only carries out economic exploitation, but is responsible for hundreds of thousands of deaths of Haitians, Salvadorans, Guatemalans and other indigenous peoples at the hands of *death squads*—trained, armed, bought and paid for by the U.S. Government.

The notion of "economic refugees" needs to be dealt with straight. *Conditions of extreme poverty and near economic collapse in the Third World countries is a political question.* Programs dictated by the International Monetary Fund and World Bank (mainly controlled by the U.S.) *". . . have helped double the gap between rich and poor countries since 1960. Resource transfers from the poor to the rich (countries) amounted to more than $400 billion from 1982 to 1990 . . . the equivalent in today's dollars of some six Marshall Plans provided by the South to the North . . . ,"* (Noam Chomsky, "The Masters of Mankind," *The Nation,* March 29, 1993). Rich countries, like the U.S., have "reaped the rewards" of the out-right robbery, exploitation and plunder of the Third World.

This war on immigrants is in fact a coordinated plan of attack by the U.S. Government as a whole.

Wilson talks about how easy it is to simply walk across the border to the U.S. Well, let's see him do it! Let's see him walk away from his family, friends and the only life he's ever known. Forced to flee for his life at the point of a gun or to prevent starvation. Not knowing if he can survive in a foreign country, with a foreign language and culture. Through a gauntlet of police and *la Migra* on both sides of the border ready to beat him down or worse, rat infested tunnels, unscrupulous smugglers and racist vigilantes *whipped up by anti-immigrant politicians like himself.* Every year, hundreds of thousands of people are arrested and deported (trying to "simply walk" across the border!). Many are held captive in INS concentration camps for months. In these concentration camps, immigrants are beaten, their due process and other legal rights are often ignored and the guards and administrators who are responsible are rarely punished.

Two reports by the human rights group Americas Watch have compared violations on the border to those in the most repressive foreign countries. A report by the American Friends Service Committee [a Quaker organization] logged more than *12,000* beatings or other serious abuses by Border Patrol agents in a *two year* period.

What does it say about a society that has no money for health care, no money for education, no money for social services and is threatening to close down hospitals—yet government at all levels has no problem finding and spending *billions* of dollars to hire more Border Patrol agents, build more INS concentration camps, hire more police and build even more jails?

Wilson supports NAFTA because it will allow the U.S. to reap super-profits from the intensified exploitation of Mexico. Wilson calls for the complete denial of basic services to immigrants in the U.S.; the taking away of all their rights and their means to survive. Then he calls for using NAFTA to tighten the U.S.'s hold on Mexico and to force the Mexican people to work for nothing. Wilson is basically saying that *"immigrants have no rights and should be treated as less than human—but the U.S. has every right to exploit the Mexican people."*

At this point we are witnessing the entire established political spectrum openly discussing their plans for a clampdown against immigrants—from Pat Buchanan to Dianne Feinstein, Barbara Boxer to Bill Clinton. The question for them is not *whether* to attack immigrants but *how*.

We say Basta ya! Enough is enough!

There is nothing good about any of these proposals and they are all deserving of the utmost contempt and defiance! These politicians aim to divide us up, the native-born from the foreign, the citizens from the subjects. The government has not just chosen to scapegoat immigrants, it is driven by a necessity and fear. A fear of a section of people for whom the government has nothing to offer except more brutal exploitation and hardship. The necessity to try to control immigrants that along with other oppressed people have risen up in rebellions in many cities across the U.S.

We need to get clear that this war on immigrants is in fact *a coordinated plan of attack by the U.S. Government as a whole*. We must learn to rely on ourselves and take matters into our own hands. Only by being bold, stepping out and taking a firm stand—*right now*—with and on the side of our immigrant sisters and brothers, will we be able to beat back and defeat this war.

This is a challenge to those of us who the government has deemed "legal," who the politicians are counting on for our complicity in their crimes against immigrants. We cannot be like the "good Germans" of two generations ago. An example for us is being set in Germany of today, where thousands of people have taken to the streets in pitched battles to confront the Nazi thugs and the German government's attacks on immigrants. Here, too, the escalating attacks on immigrants by the U.S. Government in collusion with racist vigilantes must be met by resistance in the streets. *The war on immigrants must be stopped!*

Organizations to Contact

The editors have compiled the following list of organizations concerned with the issues debated in this book. The descriptions are derived from materials provided by the organizations. All have publications or information available for interested readers. The list was compiled on the date of publication of the present volume; names, addresses, and phone numbers may change. Be aware that many organizations take several weeks or longer to respond to inquiries, so allow as much time as possible.

American Civil Liberties Union (ACLU)
132 W. 43rd St.
New York, NY 10036
(212) 944-9800
(212) 921-7916 (fax)

The ACLU is a national organization that champions the rights found in the Declaration of Independence and the U.S. Constitution. The ACLU Immigrants' Rights Project works with refugees and immigrants facing deportation, and with immigrants in the workplace. It has published reports, position papers, and a book, *The Rights of Aliens and Refugees*, that details what freedoms immigrants and refugees have under the U.S. Constitution.

American Friends Service Committee (AFSC)
1501 Cherry St.
Philadelphia, PA 19102
(215) 241-7000

The AFSC is a Quaker organization that attempts to relieve human suffering and find new approaches to world peace and social justice through nonviolence. It lobbies against what it believes to be unfair immigration laws, especially sanctions criminalizing the employment of illegal immigrants. It has published *Sealing Our Borders: The Human Toll*, a report documenting human rights violations committed by law enforcement agents against immigrants.

American Immigration Control Foundation (AICF)
PO Box 525
Monterey, VA 24465
(703) 468-2022
(703) 468-2024 (fax)

AICF is an independent research and education organization that believes massive immigration, especially illegal immigration, is harming America. It calls for an end to illegal immigration and for stricter controls on legal immigration. The foundation publishes the monthly newsletter *Border Watch* and two pamphlets: John Vinson's *Immigration Out of Control*, and Lawrence Auster's *The Path to National Suicide: An Essay on Immigration and Multiculturalism*.

American Immigration Lawyers Association (AILA)
1400 I St. NW
Washington, DC 20005
(202) 371-9377

112

AILA is a professional association of lawyers who work in the field of immigration and nationality law. It publishes the *AILA Immigration Journal* and compiles and distributes a continuously updated bibliography of government and private documents on immigration laws and regulations.

Americans for Immigration Control (AIC)
717 Second St. NE, Suite 307
Washington, DC 20002
(202) 543-3719

AIC is a lobbying organization that works to influence Congress to adopt legal reforms that would reduce U.S. immigration. It calls for increased funding for the U.S. Border Patrol and the deployment of military forces to prevent illegal immigration. It also supports sanctions against employers who hire illegal immigrants and opposes amnesty for such immigrants. AIC offers articles and brochures stating its position on immigration.

Americas Watch (AW)
485 Fifth Ave.
New York, NY 10017
(212) 972-8400
(212) 972-0905 (fax)

AW, a division of Human Rights Watch, is an organization that promotes human rights, especially for Latin Americans. It publicizes human rights violations and encourages international protests against governments responsible for them. AW has published *Brutality Unchecked: Human Rights Abuses Along the U.S. Border with Mexico.*

The Brookings Institution
1775 Massachusetts Ave. NW
Washington, DC 20036
(202) 797-6000
(202) 797-6004 (fax)

The institution, founded in 1927, is a liberal research and education organization that publishes material on economics, government, and foreign policy. It publishes analyses of immigration issues in its quarterly journal, *Brookings Review*, and in various books and reports.

Carrying Capacity Network (CCN)
1325 G St. NW, Suite 1003
Washington, DC 20005-3104
(202) 879-3044
(202) 879-3019 (fax)

The network is a coalition of individuals and organizations concerned with the interrelated issues of environmental protection, population stabilization, and resource conservation. It argues that immigration to America should be limited to ensure that the population does not exceed the nation's carrying capacity—"the number of individuals who can be supported without degrading the natural, cultural, and social environment." It frequently publishes articles on immigration policy in its quarterly journal *Focus* and its monthly newsletter *Clearinghouse Bulletin*. It also has published the widely cited study "The Net National Costs of Immigration," by Donald Huddle.

Cato Institute
1000 Massachusetts Ave. NW
Washington, DC 20001
(202) 546-0200
(202) 546-0728 (fax)

The institute is a libertarian public policy research foundation dedicated to stimulating policy debate. It believes immigration is good for the U.S. economy and favors easing immigration restrictions. As well as various articles on immigration, the institute has published Julian L. Simon's book *The Economic Consequences of Immigration.*

Center for Immigrants Rights (CIR)
48 St. Mark's Pl., 4th Fl.
New York, NY 10003
(212) 505-6890

The center offers immigrants information concerning their rights. It provides legal support, advocacy, and assistance to immigrants and strives to influence immigration policy. The center publishes fact sheets on immigrant rights and immigration law and the quarterly newsletter *CIR Report.*

Center for Immigration Studies
1815 H St. NW, Suite 1010
Washington, DC 20006-3604
(202) 466-8185

The center studies the effects of immigration on the economic, social, demographic, and environmental conditions in the United States. It believes that the large number of recent immigrants has become a burden on America and favors reforming immigration laws to make them consistent with U.S. interests. The center publishes reports, position papers, and the quarterly journal *Immigration Review.*

Federation for American Immigration Reform (FAIR)
1666 Connecticut Ave. NW, Suite 400
Washington, DC 20009
(202) 328-7004
(202) 387-3447 (fax)

FAIR works to stop illegal immigration and to limit legal immigration. It believes that the growing flood of immigrants into the United States causes higher unemployment and taxes social services. FAIR has published many reports and position papers, including *Ten Steps to Securing America's Borders* and *Immigration 2000: The Century of the New American Sweatshop.*

Foundation for Economic Education, Inc. (FEE)
30 S. Broadway
Irvington-on-Hudson, NY 10533
(914) 591-7230
(914) 591-8910 (fax)

FEE publishes information and research in support of capitalism, free trade, and limited government. It occasionally publishes articles opposing government restrictions on immigration in its monthly magazine, *The Freeman.*

The Heritage Foundation
214 Massachusetts Ave. NE
Washington, DC 20002
(202) 546-4400

The foundation is a conservative public policy research institute. It has published articles pertaining to immigration in its *Backgrounder* series and in its quarterly journal, *Policy Review*.

National Alliance Against Racist and Political Repression (NAARPR)
11 John St., Rm. 702
New York, NY 10038
(212) 406-3330
(212) 406-3542 (fax)

NAARPR is a coalition of political, labor, church, civic, student, and community organizations that oppose the many forms of human rights repression in the United States. It seeks to end the harassment and deportation of illegal immigrant workers. The alliance publishes pamphlets and a quarterly newsletter, *The Organizer*.

National Coalition of Advocates for Students (NCAS)
100 Boylston St., Suite 737
Boston, MA 02116-4610
(617) 357-8507
(617) 357-9549 (fax)

NCAS is a national network of child advocacy organizations that work on public school issues. Through its Immigrant Student Program it works to ensure that immigrants are given sufficient and appropriate education. The coalition has published two book-length reports: *New Voices: Immigrant Students in U.S. Public Schools* and *Immigrant Students: Their Legal Right of Access to Public Schools*.

National Council of La Raza (NCLR)
810 First St. NW, Suite 300
Washington, DC 20002
(202) 289-1380
(202) 289-8173 (fax)

NCLR is a national organization that seeks to improve opportunities for Americans of Hispanic descent. It conducts research on many issues, including immigration, and opposes restrictive immigration laws. The council publishes and distributes congressional testimony and reports, including *Unfinished Business: The Immigration Control and Reform Act of 1986* and *Unlocking the Golden Door: Hispanics and the Citizenship Process*.

The National Network for Immigrant and Refugee Rights
310 Eighth St., Ste. 307
Oakland, CA 94607
(510) 465-1984
(510) 465-7548 (fax)

The network includes community, church, labor, and legal groups committed to the cause of equal rights for all immigrants. These groups work to end discrimination and unfair treatment of illegal immigrants and refugees. The network aims to strengthen and coordinate educational efforts among immigration advocates nationwide. It publishes a monthly newsletter, *Network News*.

Negative Population Growth, Inc. (NPG)
PO Box 1206
Teaneck, NJ 07666-1206
(201) 837-3555
(201) 837-0270 (fax)

NPG believes that world population must be reduced and that the United States is already overpopulated. It calls for an end to illegal immigration and an annual cap on legal immigration of 200,000 people. This would achieve "zero net migration" because 200,000 people exit the country each year, according to NPG. NPG frequently publishes position papers on population and immigration in its *NPG Forum*.

El Rescate
2675 W. Olympic Blvd.
Los Angeles, CA 90006
(213) 387-3284

El Rescate provides free legal and social services to Central American refugees. It is involved in federal litigation to uphold the constitutional rights of refugees and illegal immigrants. It compiles and distributes articles and information and publishes the newsletter *El Rescate*.

La Resistencia
PO Box 2823
Houston, TX 77252-2823
(713) 662-4036

La Resistencia is an organization that combats attacks on immigrants. It believes that immigration to the United States is largely the result of U.S. foreign policies that produce poverty, starvation, and political repression abroad. It opposes aggressive immigration control efforts, the denial of public education and social services to immigrants, and popular anti-immigrant sentiments.

The Rockford Institute
934 N. Main St.
Rockford, IL 61103-7061
(815) 964-5053
(815) 965-1827 (fax)

The institute is a conservative research center that studies capitalism, religion, and liberty. It has published numerous articles questioning immigration and legalization policies in its monthly magazine *Chronicles*.

United States General Accounting Office (GAO)
441 G St. NW
Washington, DC 20548
(202) 275-2812

The GAO is the investigative arm of the U.S. Congress and is charged with examining all matters related to the receipt and disbursement of public funds. It frequently publishes reports evaluating the effectiveness of U.S. immigration policies.

Bibliography

Books

Lawrence Auster — *The Path to National Suicide: An Essay on Immigration and Multiculturalism.* Monterey, VA: American Immigration Control Foundation, 1990.

Frank D. Bean, George Vernez, and Charles B. Keely — *Opening and Closing the Doors: Evaluating Immigration Reform and Control.* Lanham, MD: University Press of America, 1989.

George J. Borjas — *Friends or Strangers: The Impact of Immigration on the U.S. Economy.* New York: Basic Books, 1990.

Vernon M. Briggs Jr. — *Mass Immigration and the National Interest.* Armonk, NY: M.E. Sharpe, 1992.

David Carliner et al. — *The Rights of Aliens and Refugees.* 2nd ed. Carbondale: Southern Illinois University Press, 1990.

Leo R. Chavez — *Shadowed Lives: Undocumented Immigrants in American Society.* Orlando, FL: Harcourt Brace Jovanovich, 1992.

Linda Chavez — *Out of the Barrio: Toward a New Politics of Hispanic Assimilation.* New York: Basic Books, 1991.

Ted Conover — *Coyotes: A Journey Through the Secret World of America's Illegal Aliens.* New York: Vintage Books, 1987.

Wayne A. Cornelius, ed. — *The Changing Role of Mexican Labor in the U.S. Economy.* La Jolla, CA: Center for U.S.-Mexican Studies, 1989.

Sergio Díaz-Briquets and Sidney Weintraub, eds. — *The Effects of Receiving Country Policies on Migration Flows.* Boulder, CO: Westview Press, 1991.

Robert W. Fox and Ira H. Mehlman — *Crowding Out the Future: World Population Growth, U.S. Immigration, and Pressures on Natural Resources.* Washington, DC: Federation for American Immigration Reform, 1992.

Lindsey Grant — *Elephants in the Volkswagen: Facing the Tough Questions About Our Overcrowded Country.* New York: W.H. Freeman, 1992.

David M. Heer — *Undocumented Mexicans in the United States.* New York: Cambridge University Press, 1990.

Daniel James — *Illegal Immigration: An Unfolding Crisis.* Lanham, MD: University Press of America, 1991.

Dan Lacey — *The Essential Immigrant.* New York: Hippocrene Books, 1990.

Eugene McCarthy — *A Colony of the World: The United States Today.* New York: Hippocrene Books, 1992.

Thomas Muller — *Immigrants and the American City.* New York: New York University Press, 1993.

Carole Nagengast, Rodolfo Stavenhagen, and Michael Kearney	*Human Rights and Indigenous Workers: The Mixtecs in Mexico and the United States.* La Jolla, CA: Center for U.S.-Mexican Studies, 1992.
Francisco L. Rivera-Batiz, Selig L. Sechzer, and Ira N. Gang, eds.	*U.S. Immigration Policy Reform in the 1980s: A Preliminary Assessment.* New York: Praeger, 1991.
Julian L. Simon	*The Economic Consequences of Immigration.* Cambridge, MA: Blackwell, 1989.
Dan Stein, ed.	*Immigration 2000: The Century of the New American Sweatshop.* Washington, DC: Federation for American Immigration Reform, 1992.
John Vinson	*Immigration Out of Control: The Interests Against America.* Monterey, VA: American Immigration Control Foundation, 1992.
Ben J. Wattenberg	*The First Universal Nation.* New York: Maxwell Macmillan International, 1991.
Daniel Wolf	*Undocumented Aliens and Crime.* La Jolla, CA: Center for U.S.-Mexican Studies, 1988.

Periodicals

Virginia D. Abernethy	"Jobs, Politics, and Immigration," *Chronicles*, October 1993. Available from PO Box 800, Mount Morris, IL 61054.
Charlotte Allen	"America: Restricted Territory," *Insight*, March 16, 1992. Available from 3600 New York Ave. NE, Washington, DC 20002.
American Friends Service Committee	*Sealing Our Borders: The Human Toll.* Third Report of the Immigration Law Enforcement Monitoring Project, February 1992. Available from 1501 Cherry St., Philadelphia, PA 19102.
Gary S. Becker	"An Open Door for Immigrants—the Auction," *The Wall Street Journal*, October 14, 1992.
Tom Bethell	"Immigration, Sí; Welfare, No," *The American Spectator*, November 1993. Available from 2020 N. 14th St., Suite 750, Arlington, VA 22216.
George J. Borjas	"Tired, Poor, on Welfare," *National Review*, December 13, 1993.
Leon F. Bouvier and John L. Martin	"Four Hundred Million Americans! The Latest Census Bureau Projections," Center for Immigration Studies *Backgrounder*, January 1993. Available from 1815 H St. NW, Suite 1010, Washington, DC 20006-3604.
Peter Brimelow	"Time to Rethink Immigration?" *National Review*, June 22, 1992.
Pat Buchanan	"America Has a Right to Preserve Its Identity," *Conservative Chronicle*, August 28, 1991. Available from PO Box 11297, Des Moines, IA 50340-1297.
Ruth Coniff	"The War on Aliens," *The Progressive*, October 1993.

The CQ Researcher	"Immigration Reform," September 24, 1993. Available from 1414 22nd St. NW, Washington, DC 20037.
Crossroads	"Immigration Today: Scapegoating Without Borders," November 1993.
Humphrey Dalton	"Help Save America," *Conservative Review*, December 1992. Available from 1307 Dolley Madison Blvd., Rm. 203, McLean, VA 22101.
Nick Ervin	"Facing the Immigration Issue," *Hi Sierran*, October 1992. Available from the Sierra Club, 3820 Ray St., San Diego, CA 92104-3623.
Richard Estrada	"The Impact of Immigration on Hispanic-Americans," *Chronicles*, July 1991.
Jaclyn Fierman	"Is Immigration Hurting the U.S.?" *Fortune*, August 9, 1993.
Francis Fukuyama	"Immigrants and Family Values," *Commentary*, May 1993.
David Gergen	"A Dreadful Mess at the INS," *U.S. News & World Report*, March 22, 1993.
Paul Glastris	"Immigration Crackdown," *U.S. News & World Report*, June 21, 1993.
Beatriz Johnston Hernandez	"Running the Gauntlet," *New Internationalist*, September 1991.
Donald L. Huddle	"Immigration, Jobs, and Wages: The Misuses of Econometrics," *The NPG Forum*, April 1992. Available from Negative Population Growth, Inc., PO Box 1206, Teaneck, NJ 07666-1206.
Donald L. Huddle	"The Net National Costs of Immigration," July 20, 1993. Available from Carrying Capacity Network, 1325 G St. NW, Suite 1003, Washington, DC 20005-3104.
Daniel James	"Close the Border to All Newcomers," *Insight*, November 22, 1993.
Ron Jefferson	"Alienation," *ABA Journal*, September 1993. Available from 750 N. Lake Shore Dr., Chicago, IL 60611.
Michael Kinsley	"Gatecrashers," *The New Republic*, December 28, 1992.
Weston Kosova	"The INS Mess," *The New Republic*, April 13, 1992.
Richard Lacayo	"Give Me Your Rich, Your Lucky . . . ," *Time*, October 14, 1991.
R.K. Lamb	"The Half-Open Door," *Liberty*, February 1993. Available from PO Box 1167, Port Townsend, WA 98368.
Melinda Liu et al.	"The New Slave Trade," *Newsweek*, June 21, 1993.
Michael J. Mandel et al.	"The Immigrants: How They're Helping to Revitalize the U.S. Economy," *Business Week*, July 13, 1992.
Elizabeth Martinez	"When No Dogs or Mexicans Are Allowed . . . ," *Z Magazine*, January 1991.
Ira H. Mehlman	"The New Jet Set," *National Review*, March 15, 1993.
Jack Miles	"Blacks vs. Browns," *The Atlantic Monthly*, October 1992.

Stephen Moore — "Give Us Your Best, Your Brightest," *Insight*, November 22, 1993.

Stephen Moore — "Immigration Policy: Open Minds on Open Borders," *Business and Society Review*, Spring 1991.

Cecilia Muñoz — "Immigration Policy: A Tricky Business," *NACLA Report on the Americas*, May 1993.

NACLA Report on the Americas — "Coming North," July 1992. Special issue on immigration.

Debbie Nathan — "A Death on the Border," *The Progressive*, March 1993.

Oscar Rechtschaffen — "The Security Nightmare: Alien Criminals and Terrorists Flood the U.S.," *Conservative Review*, July/August 1993.

Peter H. Schuck and Rogers M. Smith — "Consensual Citizenship," *Chronicles*, July 1992.

David Simcox — "Effective Enforcement of Employer Sanctions." Testimony before the Senate Committee on the Judiciary, Subcommittee on Immigration and Refugee Affairs, April 10, 1992. Available from the Center for Immigration Studies, 1815 H St. NW, Suite 1010, Washington, DC 20006-3604.

David Simcox — "The Environmental Risks of Mass Immigration," *Scope*, Fall 1992. Available from the Center for Immigration Studies.

Julian L. Simon — "The Nativists Are Wrong," *The Wall Street Journal*, August 4, 1993.

Julian L. Simon et al. — "Why Control the Borders?" *National Review*, February 1, 1993.

Trisha Smith — "Tired of Waiting: Day Laborers Organize Against Drive-By Jobs," *Third Force*, March/April 1993.

Deborah Sontag — "Rudeness Goes Public: Calls to Restrict Immigration Come from Many Quarters," *The New York Times*, December 13, 1992.

George Sunderland — "Invasion USA: The Sequel," *Conservative Review*, April 1992.

William Tamayo — "Ignoring the Constitution," *Third Force*, November/December 1993.

John Tanton and Wayne Lutton — "Welfare Costs for Immigrants," *The Social Contract*, Fall 1992. Available from 316 1/2 E. Mitchell St., Petosky, MI 49770.

United States General Accounting Office — "IRCA-Related Discrimination." Testimony before the Senate Committee on the Judiciary, Subcommittee on Immigration and Refugee Affairs, April 3, 1992. Available from PO Box 6015, Gaithersburg, MD 20877.

Martin Morse Wooster — "Coming to America," *Reason*, November 1991.

The World & I — "The Challenge of Immigration" (Special Report), October 1992. Available from 2800 New York Ave. NE, Washington, DC 20002.

The World & I — "Immigration: Boon or Bane to the U.S.?" January 1994.

Index